Alcohol and Public Policy

Alcohol and its consumption is a major topic for public policy-making. Growing awareness of alcohol-related health problems among the general public has led to high levels of interest in alcohol consumption and its impact on society. This innovative collection of new perspectives on this critically important issue is informed by a leading group of international social scientists. Topics covered include alcoholism, the family, minimum pricing, paternalistic controls, and Socially Responsible Investment programs. Together, these essays reveal illuminating new insights into how public policy might be improved.

This book was originally published as a special issue of *Contemporary Social Science*.

Thom Brooks is Professor of Law and Government at Durham University, UK, and the founding editor of the *Journal of Moral Philosophy*. His current research interests include criminal law and justice, citizenship and immigration, global justice and human rights, sentencing and public policy more generally.

Contemporary Issues in Social Science

Series editor: David Canter, University of Huddersfield, UK

Contemporary Social Science, the journal of the **Academy of Social Sciences**, is an interdisciplinary, cross-national journal which provides a forum for disseminating and enhancing theoretical, empirical and/or pragmatic research across the social sciences and related disciplines. Reflecting the objectives of the Academy of Social Sciences, it emphasises the publication of work that engages with issues of major public interest and concern across the world, and highlights the implications of that work for policy and professional practice.

The *Contemporary Issues in Social Science* book series contains the journal's most cutting-edge special issues. Leading scholars compile thematic collections of articles that are linked to the broad intellectual concerns of *Contemporary Social Science*, and as such these special issues are an important contribution to the work of the journal. The series editor works closely with the guest editor(s) of each special issue to ensure they meet the journal's high standards. The main aim of publishing these special issues as a series of books is to allow a wider audience of both scholars and students from across multiple disciplines to engage with the work of *Contemporary Social Science* and the Academy of Social Sciences.

Titles in the series:

Crowds in the 21st Century
Perspectives from contemporary social science
Edited by John Drury and Clifford Stott

Biologising the Social Sciences
Challenging Darwinian and Neuroscience Explanations
Edited by David Canter and David Turner

The Social Dynamics of Web 2.0
Interdisciplinary Perspectives
Edited by Charalambos Tsekeris and Ioannis Katerelos

Alcohol and Public Policy
Edited by Thom Brooks

Alcohol and Public Policy

Edited by
Thom Brooks

Routledge
Taylor & Francis Group
LONDON AND NEW YORK

ACADEMY of SOCIAL SCIENCES

First published 2015
by Routledge
2 Park Square, Milton Park, Abingdon, Oxon, OX14 4RN, UK

and by Routledge
711 Third Avenue, New York, NY 10017, USA

Routledge is an imprint of the Taylor & Francis Group, an informa business

British Library Cataloguing in Publication Data
A catalogue record for this book is available from the British Library

ISBN: 978-0-415-73024-2

Typeset in Times New Roman
by RefineCatch Limited, Bungay, Suffolk

Publisher's Note
The publisher accepts responsibility for any inconsistencies that may have arisen during the conversion of this book from journal articles to book chapters, namely the possible inclusion of journal terminology.

Contents

Citation Information

The chapters in this book were originally published in *Contemporary Social Science*, volume 8, issue 1 (February 2013). When citing this material, please use the original page numbering for each article, as follows:

Chapter 4
Socially Responsible Investment in the alcohol industry: an assessment of investor attitudes and ethical arguments
Boudewijn de Bruin
Contemporary Social Science, volume 8, issue 1 (February 2013) pp. 58–70

Chapter 5
Two decades and a Category 5 hurricane later . . . tracking homeless substance abusers in New Orleans
Rachel L. Rayburn
Contemporary Social Science, volume 8, issue 1 (February 2013) pp. 18–30

Chapter 6
Alcohol and the family
Woody Caan
Contemporary Social Science, volume 8, issue 1 (February 2013) pp. 8–17

Chapter 7
The borders of booze Britain: alcohol controls and nationality
Tom Henri
Contemporary Social Science, volume 8, issue 1 (February 2013) pp. 36–45

Chapter 8
Minimum pricing for alcohol: a Millian perspective
Ben Saunders
Contemporary Social Science, volume 8, issue 1 (February 2013) pp. 71–82

Chapter 9
Respectable drinkers, sensible drinking, serious leisure: single-malt whisky enthusiasts and the moral panic of irresponsible Others
Karl Spracklen
Contemporary Social Science, volume 8, issue 1 (February 2013) pp. 46–57

Chapter 10

Storytelling: Walter Benjamin and recovery from alcoholism
Joel C. Beaupre
Contemporary Social Science, volume 8, issue 1 (February 2013) pp. 31–35

Please direct any queries you may have about the citations to clsuk.permissions@cengage.com

Notes on Contributors

Joel C. Beaupre began a serious study of recovery and alcoholism in 2006. He received his PhD in Philosophy from Vanderbilt University, USA, in 2010, having written about suffering and the Book of Job. He currently lives and teaches in Nashville, Tennessee, USA.

Thom Brooks is Professor of Law and Government at Durham University in the Durham Law School, UK. Brooks is also an Associate in Philosophy and member of the Senior Common Room at University College, Durham, UK. He works in the areas of ethics, law and public policy. His recent books include *Punishment* (2012) and *Hegel's Political Philosophy* (2d, 2013). Brooks is an Academician of the Academy of Social Sciences, Fellow of the Royal Historical Society, Fellow of the Royal Society of Arts and the founding editor of the *Journal of Moral Philosophy*.

Boudewijn de Bruin is Professor of financial ethics at the University of Groningen, The Netherlands. De Bruin studied mathematics and philosophy in Amsterdam, Berkeley and Harvard Business School, and obtained a PhD from the Institute for Logic, Language and Computation of the University of Amsterdam in 2004. De Bruin has published widely in journals such as *Law and Philosophy*, *Journal of Political Philosophy*, *Journal of Business Ethics* and *Philosophy of the Social Sciences* and is the author of *Explaining games: The epistemic programme in game theory* (2010) and *Ethics in finance: Epistemic virtues for banks, clients, raters and regulators* (2013).

Woody Caan has been involved in a variety of alcohol-related projects since 1988, when he became a Lecturer in addictive behaviour at St. George's Hospital, UK. Currently he is Professorial Fellow at the Royal Society for Public Health, Honorary Consultant to Essex County Council and a practitioner-academician in the Academy of Social Sciences.

Tom Henri studied sociology, social policy and social work at the University of Southampton, UK. He then worked as a social worker and a social work educator before taking up a lectureship at Goldsmiths, University of London, UK. His academic and research interests include the construction of youth as a problem, racisms, substance misuse, and how discourses of social class and nationality both inform and are reproduced by and through social work and social policy.

Rachel L. Rayburn is an Assistant Professor of Public Policy at Indiana University Purdue University – Fort Wayne (IPFW), USA. She holds a BS degree from Florida State University, USA, and a PhD in Sociology from The University of Central Florida, USA. Dr Rayburn teaches courses in criminal justice, law and public policy. Her current research examines desistance among homeless substance abusers. She has published articles on homelessness, drugs, and desistance from crime that have appeared in journals such as *Deviant Behavior*, *Applied Social Science*, *Society*, *The Journal of Long Term Home Health Care*, and *Sociology Health Review*.

Ben Saunders is a lecturer in Philosophy at the University of Stirling, UK. He is interested in most areas of political philosophy and normative/applied ethics, but his main research interests to date lie in democratic theory and the thought of John Stuart Mill. He has published in these areas in various journals, including *Ethics*, *Utilitas*, *Politics*, *Philosophy and Economics*, and *Political Studies*.

Karl Spracklen is a Professor of Leisure Studies at Leeds Metropolitan University, UK. He is the Chair of the Leisure Studies Association and Co-Convenor of the British Sociological Association Alcohol Study Group. His book, *Constructing Leisure* (2011), explores the history of and philosophy of leisure, including the importance of drinking and eating as leisure.

Daniel Yalisove is an Emeritus Professor at John Jay College, CUNY, USA.

Foreword

Hardly any TV drama is complete without a scene of merriment fuelled by alcohol or a character destroyed by it. This reflects the way intoxicating drinks make up the fabric of our society. So much so that if religions want to distinguish themselves from the social mass they will often use a ban on alcoholic consumption as a key pointer. Imbibing beer and wine, spirits and aperitifs is very much a social process. This means that any commercial or political attempts to deal with the many problems alcohol causes should be based on sound social science.

Consequently, this volume, edited by Thom Brooks, Professor of Law and Government at Durham University, offers an important and often overlooked perspective on public policy towards alcohol consumption. Brooks is a moral philosopher working in areas of jurisprudence. So it is particularly impressive that he has pulled together social science explorations of alcohol rather than limiting himself totally to considerations of the abstractions of ethics and the law. His careful placement of alcohol intake within the social processes raises both theoretical and practical challenges.

The problem is that research continues to make clear the conflict between the use of alcohol and its effects. It is well established that many forms of criminal violence, inside and outside the home, are fuelled by intoxication. This has been related to the way alcohol impairs cognitive skills and increases risk taking and aggression. Indeed, one recent study showed that minor crime increased by 5% and violent crime by 10% just when Sunday sales of alcohol were allowed. In addition, the medical consequences, beyond those that result from increased risk taking and violence, are also now well established.

But against this background of the disastrous effect of the demon drink, known throughout history, is its near universal use in religious and social ceremonies and leisure activities. Banning alcohol is thus clearly not an option, as became so apparent in the US prohibition era. Social science points to the need to manage alcohol consumption, and that is where the details of the ethical, sociological and psychological arguments take on particular significance.

One starting point for understanding the management of alcohol is to recognise its key role in family activities. Woody Caan's chapter in the present volume draws on personal experience and extensive research to argue the need to understand how alcohol can both help and destroy family life. A little tongue in cheek, he suggests that weddings would probably disappear if the diverse groups brought together for such gatherings were not able to damp down their social anxieties using the anxiolytic action of alcohol. The ways in which family dynamics can sustain long-term dependence on alcohol and pass that on to subsequent generations has to be put into any consideration of how to help control these destructive processes.

These complexities reveal the difficulty of finding any simple solution for reducing the problems created by alcohol abuse. Professor de Bruin, who has the much needed Chair in Financial Ethics at the University of Groningen, contributes to the present volume by exploring whether socially responsible investment is one way of reducing the sources of alcohol by limiting the funds available to the industry. However, his careful ethical analysis shows that just encouraging shareholders to make moral decisions about whether to invest in companies that produce and sell intoxicating beverages can be rather confused and often has a very shaky moral basis to it. Unless it has some very clear religious or related ideological foundation it can really not be defended. But that is the essence of temperance societies over the ages, which will only ever have a limited appeal.

Another approach, very much in the public agenda, is minimum pricing for alcohol. The Scottish government has proposed this as a way of tackling the endemic abuse of alcohol in that country. Ben Saunders from the University of Stirling explores this and looks at what the arguments are both for and against minimum pricing. As you might expect of a philosopher, he claims that the ethical arguments are weak and confused, but that it is perfectly reasonable, and indeed ethical, for governments to use increased pricing as a means of raising revenue!

Saunders even takes the argument further and suggests that the symbolic qualities of minimum pricing could contribute to a definition of national identity, distinguishing Scotland from its southern neighbour. But the Westminster government is also seriously considering minimum pricing in the light of research that indicates such a financial burden does reduce alcohol consumption, possibly reducing it most in problem drinkers. So the nationalist benefits may consequently be reduced by England's following Scotland's lead.

Managing alcohol consumption has been a recurring challenge over the centuries. It raises ethical, political, financial and social dilemmas. These can only be solved by understanding how they all interact and, further, by accepting that there is no simple, single solution. This volume therefore makes a prescient contribution to an age-old debate by drawing together a range of social perspectives.

Professor David Canter
Editor, *Contemporary Social Science*

Introduction

Thom Brooks

Introduction

Alcohol and its consumption is a major topic for public policy-making. Increases in public debate have come about by the growing awareness of the alcohol-related health problems among the general public. This topic raises difficult questions about the regulation of alcohol. When should the state regulate alcohol distribution and consumption? How should public policy balance individual freedoms and general welfare?

This book focuses on alcohol and public policy bringing together recently published essays and newly commissioned chapters never before published. Contributing authors offer and defend new critical analyses of where policies have been ineffective while illuminating more promising future strategies. The next section offers an overview of the leading contemporary research on the topic and insights into the leading issues. The following section discusses the new research presented in this issue. Social scientists have much to contribute to addressing alcohol and public policy. This issue seeks to make clear how social science might improve policy-making in this important area.

Research overview

Contemporary social science research may be broadly understood through three different lenses. The first addresses the specific ethical considerations arising from a cultural and historical perspective (Eber, 2000; Gamburd, 2008; Mancall, 1995; Robinson & Kenyon, 2009; Rorabaugh, 1979; Tracy, 2007; Tracy & Acker, 2004). Alcohol consumption is a part of many world cultures playing roles in religious or social ceremonies and celebrations as well as leisure activities (Gately, 2008). This approach has relevance for policy-makers in helping to illuminate the difficulty of drawing clear lines about where regulation should be implemented. For example, if alcohol consumption has a recreational importance for many citizens, how should policy-makers balance these interests with promoting public health and other social goods?

A second perspective focuses on the cognitive and psychological effects of alcohol in terms of human functioning and its relation to ethical considerations (Agarwal & Seitz, 2001; Feinstein, Richter, & Foster, 2012; Greenfield, Harford, & Tam, 2009; Reed, 1985; Yalisove, 2004). These effects are one source of important concern regarding the possibility and perhaps urgency of alcohol regulation. For example, it is highly relevant to understand how alcohol may impair individual judgement concerning dispositions to risk and violence (George, Rogers, & Duka, 2005; George et al., 2009; MacArthur et al., 2012; Ogle & Miller, 2004; Van Oorsouw & Merckelbach, 2012). Thus, if such links are confirmed, how the related risks might then be best managed?

Social scientists have also enriched our understanding about the effects of alcohol consumption and how this should inform public policy considerations (Babor et al., 2010; Cook, 2007).

This third perspective seeks to uncover the best methods of avoiding harm. For example, alcohol consumption has often been linked with increased rates of violence (Boden, Fergusson, & Horwood, 2012; McKnight, 2002; Martin, 2001, 2009; Pihl & Sutton, 2009). Social scientists help to identify how public policy might assist harm prevention correlated to problem drinking (Bucholz & Robins, 1989; Crombie, Irvine, Elliott, & Wallace, 2007; Graham et al., 2011; Rossow, 2001; Toomey & Wagenaar, 1999; Wilson, Gunasekara, & Thomson, 2011). Specific politic recommendations include increasing the amount of taxation levied on alcohol as a policy likely to lead to reduced crime due to intoxication (Kleiman & Heussler, 2011). Furthermore, this policy might also reduce alcohol-related disease mortality (Delcher, Maldonado- Molina, & Wagenaar, 2012) and improve public health more generally (Daley, Stahre, Chaloupka, & Naimi, 2012).

This research is relevant to other policy areas, such as criminal justice. One example is identifying the causal relation between alcohol consumption and crime (Popovici, Homer, Fang, & French, 2012). Social scientists have confirmed links between the density of alcohol establishments and violent (Toomey et al., 2012a), non-violent crime (Toomey et al., 2012b), and domestic violence (Livingston, 2011). Social scientists have also confirmed links between binge drinking and sexual assault (Abbey, 2002; Franklin, 2011; Mouilso, Fischer, & Calhoun, 2012; Rothman, Reyes, Johnson, & LaValley, 2012). There is also a link suggested between relaxation of alcohol sale restrictions and crime. One study found that minor crime increased by 5% and alcohol-driven violent crime increased by 10% when sales of alcohol were permitted on Sunday (Heaton, 2012). These findings do not necessitate a ban on alcohol distribution and consumption, but they do help to illuminate a crucial policy-related evidence pertaining to the links between alcohol, public health, and criminal justice issues to name a few.

This evidence must be understood in context. One context is sociological: for example, what roles does alcohol play in the everyday lives of many citizens and how might this be affected by new public policies in this area? A second context is normative, such as the meaning of 'harm' relevant to public policy decision-making. Both contexts are critical. Thus, if a policy change would criminalise the everyday conduct of most citizens, then this may be justified but it should require that a higher threshold of justification is satisfied. Such a change would not be trivial and should demand a more robust foundation. The legal requirement that car passengers wear seatbelts is perhaps a useful example. This may be a case where many citizens were not using seatbelts, so the change in law required a change in our everyday lives. However, seatbelt requirements still permit car passengers to travel without further restriction representing a minor, but important, legal demand meant to reduce the risk of serious harm or death in car accidents. This case is very different from criminalising alcohol consumption as the restriction of individual liberty is greater.

The normative context is also critical to understanding relevant public policy reforms. The widespread appeals to a standard of 'harm' provide a useful example. Harm has been traditionally understood in terms of the 'harm principle' as first defended by John Stuart Mill:

> That the only purpose for which power can be rightfully exercised over any member of a civilised community, against his will, is to prevent harm to others. His own good, either physical or moral, is not a sufficient warrant. He cannot rightfully be compelled to do or forbear because it will be better for him to do so, because it will make him happier, because, in the opinions of others, to do so would be wise, or even right. (1989, p. 13)

For Mill, freedom consists in our not being restrained or coerced by others so long as we do not contribute or substantially threaten harm to others. This so-called 'negative' view of freedom has won widespread support (Berlin, 1993, pp. 34 – 43). Nevertheless, this model has been subjected to serious challenges. For example, the harm principle is clear that our policies should always aim to prevent harm as a wrongful coercion. But what if we consent to harm? The prize fighter in a boxing match engages in an activity in which fellow participants may be harmed or even killed, but yet this is a species of harm for many that should be regulated although not banned.

Should then 'harm' be understood as a 'harm to autonomy'? This would avoid criminalising prize fighting under most circumstances, but raise new and serious questions about alcohol and public policy. Alcohol consumption often restricts autonomy even where persons are not legally under the influence. Does such a restriction on our autonomous capacities represent a harm even when we choose to drink? Some philosophers, such as Thomas Hill Green, argue in favour. He says:

> When we speak of freedom as something to be so highly prized, we mean a positive power or capacity of doing or enjoying something worth doing or enjoying, and that, too, something that we do or enjoy in common with others. (Green, 1986, p. 199)

The problem with permitting alcohol consumption is that, for Green, it impedes our general freedom and harms us in providing a barrier to our making 'the best of ourselves' and our faculties (1986, p. 201). Prohibition is justified on the simple ground of the recognised right on the part of society to prevent men from doing as they like, if, in the exercise of their peculiar tastes in doing as they like, they create a social nuisance. There is no right to freedom in the purchase and sale of a particular commodity, if the general result of allowing such freedom is to detract from freedom in the higher sense, from the general power of men to make the best of themselves (Green, 1986, p. 210).

There is a powerful challenge to contemporary society in these remarks. If we permit alcohol consumption and distribution, then we have a responsibility to consider the implications of such a policy in areas such as criminal justice and public health among many others. Therefore, we have a responsibility to consider how best to regulate alcohol consumption and distribution in light of the established, relevant social science evidence. We must consider the sociological and normative contexts – and come to a view about how much risk is acceptable. Perhaps, most readers will agree that Green is overcautious (e.g. prohibition is not necessary to secure a satisfactory level of freedom) and overambitious (e.g. public policy-makers need not be required to focus on how all individuals must achieve perfectionism, but rather how policy might satisfy demands of political justice) (Brooks, 2003).

New research

This book includes new research about alcohol and public policy that is briefly reviewed below. It raises new questions and offers more penetrating insights produced by leading international researchers.

De Bruin (2013) addresses the issue of socially responsible investment (SRI). SRI involves ethical decision-making by shareholders regarding industries for potential future investment.

SRI investors have often excluded the alcohol industry. The relevant question is why this is the case and de Bruin examines three separate positions. The first is the public goods argument: the idea is that SRI investors should focus on improving the public goods of society where possible. The concern is that investment in the alcohol industry might be counterproductive to this aim and, therefore, SRI investors should avoid this industry altogether. De Bruin convincingly argues that this position does not withstand close scrutiny. He states that public goods are highly contested and it is not certain that any investment in the alcohol industry would contravene public goods. Furthermore, there is an issue concerning democratic accountability if institutional, but not individual, investors determined a society's public goods.

A second argument is the religious values argument, which says that SRI should be guided by the religious values of investors. De Bruin finds this as a more coherent position than the public goods argument, but its problem is that it runs the risk of possibly imposing a particular set of religious values on others given the reasonable pluralism that characterises modern societies (Brooks & Nussbaum, 2015; Rawls, 1996).

The final position considered is what de Bruin calls the ethical issues argument. This is the view that investors might be led by particular ethical commitments and use these moral norms to determine investment choice. This position avoids the problem of public good selection because it does not prioritise any such goods. However, the ethical issues argument might lend a greater support to concerned investors obtaining powers as activist shareholders in alcohol corporations to better promote favoured ethical commitments. Thus, SRI should not exclude the alcohol industry, but rather it ought to engage more closely with the industry.

One leading policy proposal for reducing alcohol consumption is minimum pricing per unit. The latest proposal has been developed in Scotland by the Scottish National Party (SNP). Saunders (2013) considers this proposal from the perspective of John Stuart Mill's views about political justice. Mill (1989) argues that the state may legitimately interfere in the conduct of citizens in order to prevent harm. Saunders argues that Mill's views might lend some support to certain restrictions, such as minimum age requirements or health warnings, but they would stop well short of prohibition and including a rejection of minimum pricing schemes. Curiously, Mill did not oppose the use of taxation to raise state revenues: his views might then support an added tax on alcohol to raise revenue, but not for the purpose of deterring individuals from alcohol consumption. This latter purpose is not legitimate because it is a violation of individual liberty. So, perhaps, the SNP might move forward with its policy plans, but they cannot for the reasons they offer if to avoid running afoul of Mill's views on justice.

A particular site of neglected attention by public policy-makers is the family. It is widely recognised that family members may bear high costs and risks, but without any clear systematic approach for how the family might be better understood in this context. Caan (2013) offers a wide-ranging analysis that presents a powerful case for the value of better understanding the importance of family ties and how they might improve policy-making in this area.

Rayburn (2013) considers a different case study for the critical examination. This is the case of homeless substance abusers in New Orleans. The focus is on the New Orleans Homeless Substance Abusers Program, which employs a three-stage treatment programme of detoxification, transitional care, and independent living. This careful study not only reveals the many obstacles confronting the successful implementation of such programmes, but also the importance of establishing and maintaining social bonding to assist desistance.[1]

Another chapter considers alcohol controls from an international perspective. We revisit the issue of minimum pricing in historical and comparative contexts. Henri (2013) argues that alcohol controls may be utilised to reinforce notions of nationality. Therefore, we should not only consider these controls strictly in terms of public health, but also in reference to identity. Historically, alcohol control has been used to further define notions of 'us' and 'them'. For example, prohibition in the USA arose, in part, in response by a dominant Protestant majority to large influx of Catholic immigrants. Henri (2013) challenges us to consider that contemporary attempts at alcohol controls in places such as Scotland may be an attempt to further define Scotland's national identity, namely, the idea of Scottishness versus that of 'others'. Alcohol controls may not only speak to the effectiveness of public policy, but also be expressive about the self-identity of groups. This is an important dimension that is easily overlooked, but usefully illuminated in this thought-provoking piece.

This book contains two chapters never before published. The first is by Thom Brooks and examines alcohol, risk and public policy. Alcohol consumption is often linked with risky behaviour, including criminal activities. But alcohol is also an important part of celebrations. So how can balance risks best without banning alcohol consumption? Brooks considers the criminal law and argues it is a blunt instrument and requires further policy measures. He then examines the use of taxes, such as increased taxes on the sale of alcohol per unit, but finds this also a crude and difficult instrument to achieve policy outcomes balancing risks. Instead, Brooks favours the use of nudges and insights from behavioural economics about how we can get this balance right with several new policy proposals for how this could be implemented.

A second previously unpublished essay is by Daniel Yalisove, who examines research in the United States concerning alcohol and other drug (AOD) policy. Yalisove surveys the rich sources of data in the USA on AOD use across federal and state programmes. He then provides an illuminating account of substance abuse treatment programmes in the USA, but also into assistance beyond these treatment programmes. Yalisove notes emergent trends in treatment and prevention issues before providing several policy proposals with potentially significant future outcomes in a wide-ranging and authoritative study.

Conclusion

Alcohol has become a challenging issue for policy-makers. Social scientists have made significant contributions to our understanding of the wider context, establishing crucial links between alcohol and areas of policy concern, such as criminal justice and public health. This new book extends this body of research knowledge to provide us with new critical analyses of existing policies and how they might be improved in future. The evidence is clear that the social science matters as a field of study that illuminates and has policy relevance.

Note

1. See Brooks (2012) on the importance of social bonding to assist desistance more generally.

References

Abbey, A. (2002). Alcohol-related sexual assault: A common problem among college students. *Journal of Studies on Alcohol*, *14*, 118–128.

Agarwal, D., & Seitz, H. K. (Eds.). (2001). *Alcohol in health and disease*. New York: M. Dekker.

Babor, T. F., Caetano, R., Casswell, S., Edwards, G., Giesbrecht, N., Graham, K. et al. (2010). *Alcohol: No ordinary commodity. Research and public policy*. Oxford: Oxford University Press.

Berlin, I. (1993). Two concepts of liberty. In D. Miller (Ed.), *Liberty* (pp. 33–57). Oxford: Oxford University Press.

Boden, J. M., Fergusson, D. M., & Horwood, L. J. (2012). Alcohol misuse and violent behavior: Findings from a 30-year longitudinal study. *Drug and Alcohol Dependence*, *122*, 135–141.

Brooks, T. (2003). T. H. Green's theory of punishment. *History of Political Thought*, *24*, 685–701.

Brooks, T. (2012). *Punishment*. London: Routledge.

Brooks, T., & Nussbaum, M. C. (Eds.). (2015). *Rawls's political liberalism*. New York, NY: Columbia University Press.

de Bruin, B. (2013). Socially responsible investment in the alcohol industry: An assessment of investor attitudes and ethical arguments. *Contemporary Social Science*, *8*, 58–70.

Bucholz, K. K., & Robins, L. N. (1989). Sociological research on alcohol use, problems, and policy. *Annual Review of Sociology*, *15*, 163–186.

Caan, W. (2013). Alcohol and the family. *Contemporary Social Science*, *8*, 8–17.

Cook, P. J. (2007). *Paying the tab: The economics of alcohol policy*. Princeton, NJ: Princeton University Press.

Crombie, I., Irvine, L., Elliott, L., & Wallace, H. (2007). How do public health policies tackle alcohol-related harm: A review of 12 developed countries. *Alcohol and Alcoholism*, *42*, 492–499.

Daley, J. I., Stahre, M. A., Chaloupka, F. J., & Naimi, T. S. (2012). The impact of a 25-cent-per-drink alcohol tax increase. *American Journal of Preventive Medicine, 42*, 382–389.

Delcher, C., Maldonado-Molina, M. M., & Wagenaar, A. C. (2012). Effects of alcohol taxes on alcohol-related disease mortality in New York state from 1969 to 2006. *Addictive Behaviors, 37*, 783–789.

Eber, C. (2000). *Women and alcohol in a highland Maya town: Water of hope, water of sorrow*. Austin, TX: University of Texas Press.

Feinstein, E. C., Richter, L., & Foster, S. E. (2012). Addressing the critical health problem of adolescent substance abuse through health care, research, and public policy. *Journal of Adolescent Health, 50*, 431–436.

Franklin, C. A. (2011). An investigation of the relationship between self-control and alcohol-induced sexual assault victimization. *Criminal Justice and Behavior, 38*, 263–285.

Gamburd, M. R. (2008). *Breaking the ashes: The culture of illicit liquor in Sri Lanka*. Ithaca, NY: Cornell University Press.

Gately, I. (2008). *Drink: A cultural history of alcohol*. New York, NY: Gotham.

George, S., Rogers, R. D., & Duka, T. (2005). The acute effect of alcohol on decision making in social drinkers. *Psychopharmacology, 182*, 160–169.

George, W. H., Davis, K. C., Norris, J., Heiman, J. R., Stoner, S. A., Schacht, R. L. et al. (2009). Indirect effects of acute alcohol intoxification on sexual risk-taking: The roles of subjective and physiological sexual arousal. *Archives of Sexual Behavior, 38*, 498–513.

Graham, K., Bernards, S., Knibbe, R., Kairouz, S., Kuntsche, S., Wilsnack, S.C. et al. (2011). Alcohol-related negative consequences among drinkers around the world. *Addiction, 106*, 1391–1405.

Green, T. H. (1986). Lecture on 'Liberal legislation and freedom of contract'. In P. Harris & J. Morrow (Eds.), *Lectures on the principles of political obligation and other writings* (pp. 194–212). Cambridge: Cambridge University Press.

Greenfield, T. K., Harford, T. C., & Tam, T. W. (2009). Modeling cognitive influences on drinking and alcohol problems. *Journal of Studies on Alcohol and Drugs, 70*, 78–86.

Heaton, P. (2012). Sunday liquor laws and crime. *Journal of Public Economics, 96*, 42–52.

Henri, T. (2013). The borders of Booze Britain: Alcohol controls and nationality. *Contemporary Social Science, 8*, 36–45.

Kleiman, M. A. R., & Heussler, L. (2011). Crime-minimizing drug policy. *Journal of Criminal Justice, 39*, 286–288.

Livingston, M. (2011). A longitudinal analysis of alcohol outlet density and domestic violence. *Addiction, 106*, 919–925.

MacArthur, G. J., Smith, M. C., Melotti, R., Heron, J., Macleod, J., Hickman, M. et al. (2012). Patterns of alcohol use and multiple risk behaviour by gender during early and late adolescence: The ALSPAC cohort. *Journal of Public Health, 34*, 120–130.

McKnight, D. (2002). *From hunting to drinking: The devastating effects of alcohol on an Australian aboriginal community*. London: Routledge.

Mancall, P. C. (1995). *Deadly medicine: Indians and alcohol in early America*. Ithaca, NY: Cornell University Press.

Martin, A. L. (2001). *Alcohol, sex, and gender in late medieval and early modern Europe*. Basingstoke: Palgrave Macmillan.

Martin, A. L. (2009). *Alcohol, violence, and disorder in traditional Europe*. Kirksville, MI: Truman State University Press.

Mill, J. S. (1989). *On liberty and other writings*. Cambridge: Cambridge University Press.

Mouilso, E. R., Fischer, S., & Calhoun, K. S. (2012). A prospective study of sexual assault and alcohol use among first-year college women. *Violence and Victims, 27*, 78–94.

Ogle, R. L., & Miller, W. R. (2004). The effects of alcohol intoxication and gender on the social information processing of hostile provocations involving male and female provocateurs. *Journal of Studies on Alcohol and Drugs, 65*, 54–62.

Pihl, R. O., & Sutton, R. (2009). Drugs and aggression readily mix: So what now? *Substance Use & Misuse, 44*, 1188–1203.

Popovici, I., Homer, J. F., Fang, H., & French, M. T. (2012). Alcohol use and crime: Findings from a longitudinal sample of U.S. adolescents and young adults. *Alcoholism – Clinical and Experimental Research, 36*, 532–543.

Rawls, J. (1996). *Political liberalism* (paperback ed.). New York, NY: Columbia University Press.

Rayburn, R. L. (2013). Two decades and a category five hurricane later . . . tracking homeless substance abusers in New Orleans. *Contemporary Social Science, 8*, 18–30.

Reed, M. (1985). The myth of 'the average alcohol response'. *Alcohol, 2*, 515–519.

Robinson, S., & Kenyon, A. L. (2009). *Ethics in the alcohol industry*. Basingstoke: Palgrave Macmillan.

Rorabaugh, W. J. (1979). *The alcoholic republic: An American tradition*. Oxford: Oxford University Press.

Rossow, I. (2001). Alcohol and homicide: A cross-cultural comparison of the relationship in 14 European countries. *Addiction, 96*, 77–92.

Rothman, E. F., Reyes, L. M., Johnson, R. M., & LaValley, M. (2012). Does the alcohol make them do it? Dating violence perpetration and drinking among youth. *Epidemiologic Reviews, 34*, 103–119.

Saunders, B. (2013). Minimum pricing for alcohol: A Millian perspective. *Contemporary Social Science, 8*, 71–82.

Toomey, T. L., Erickson, D. J., Carlin, B. P., Lenk, K. M., Quick, H. S., Jones, A. M.et al. (2012a). The association between density of alcohol establishments and violent crime within urban neighborhoods. *Alcoholism – Clinical and Experimental Research, 36*, 1468–1473.

Toomey, T. L., Erickson, D. J., Carlin, B. P., Quick, H. S., Harwood, E. M., Lenk, K. M. et al. (2012b). Is the density of alcohol establishments related to nonviolent crime? *Journal of Studies on Alcohol and Drugs, 73*, 21–25.

Toomey, T. L., & Wagenaar, A. C. (1999). Policy options for prevention: The case of alcohol. *Journal of Public Health Policy, 20*, 192–213.

Tracy, S. W. (2007). *Alcoholism in America: From reconstruction to prohibition*. Baltimore, MD: Johns Hopkins University Press.

Tracy, S. W., & Acker, C. J. (Eds.). (2004). *Altering American consciousness: The history of alcohol and drug use in the United States, 1800–2000*. Amherst, MA: University of Massachusetts Press.

Van Oorsouw, K., & Merckelbach, H. (2012). The effects of alcohol on crime-related memories: A field study. *Applied Cognitive Psychology, 26*, 82–90.

Wilson, N., Gunasekara, I., & Thomson, G. (2011). The benefits and harms of alcohol use in New Zealand: What politicians might consider. *New Zealand Medical Journal, 124*, 85–89.

Yalisove, D. (2004). *Introduction to alcohol research: Implications for treatment, prevention and policy*. Boston, MA: Pearson.

Research and US AOD policy

Daniel Yalisove, PhD

Introduction

Having just surveyed the enormous research literature for a book on substance abuse in the USA with Danielle Barry, in this chapter, I plan to write a brief summary of findings with commentary. First, I will outline the US federal and state administrative structure regarding alcohol and other drug (AOD) research and policy. Then I will highlight the research findings of particular salience with some recommendations for treatment, prevention, and policy. I conclude with some commentary in which I discuss the challenges of properly summarising, distilling, and translating this enormous body of research so that it can be translated into practical issues in treatment, prevention, and policy. I will make a preliminary assessment of two federal agencies that have a role in this process, the Clinical Trials Network (CTN) and the addiction technology transfer centers (ATTC). I will make recommendations for US drug policy, treatment, and prevention based on the latest research and current trends.

Current US administrative structure regarding AOD research and policy

Much of the impetus for AOD research in the USA has come from two federal agencies, now a part of Substance Abuse and Mental Health Services Administration (SAMHSA), the National Institute on Drug Abuse (NIDA), and the National Institute on Alcoholism and Alcohol Abuse (NIAAA). In addition to doing research themselves, they fund outside research, and publish technical and non-technical reports on research findings. SAMHSA supports the Empirically Supported Interventions (ESI) movement though the creation of National Registry of Evidence-based Programs and Practices (NREPP) and funding the ATTCs and CTN mentioned above.

These bureaucracies also advise on policy regarding drug and alcohol regulation and must support the current federal drug laws. The federal policy on drugs is largely prohibitionistic and has been so for many years. Drugs with no known medical use are prohibited. Those medications with high addictive potential are tightly regulated. Unsanctioned possession or distribution of these drugs is illegal under US federal regulations. Regarding alcohol and tobacco, which are legal in the USA, NIAAA and NIDA support research on the effectiveness of various regulations on their use and intervention for those who should not use these substances or want to quit.

While NIDA and NIAAA have sponsored research initiatives and promote various policies on AOD, each state regulates the sale of alcohol and tobacco and regulate substance abuse treatment as a consequence of large federal grants that delegated states money to create their own substance abuse agencies in the 1980s. Individual states may have policies that may not be in concert with federal agency policies. The differing policies between the federal and states' position on marijuana is the most obvious example.

It should be noted that Alcoholics Anonymous has had a strong impact on US alcohol treatment policy on both the federal and state levels since the 1950s (Yalisove, 1998). Historically this came through the National Council on Alcoholism. This organisation ultimately evolved into the medical speciality for treating addiction, the American Society of Addiction Medicine (ASAM) and while still congenial to AA, is no longer linked to AA's views on alcoholism the way the National Council on Alcoholism was.

Brief summary of research findings on AOD

Epidemiology

The USA has a rich ongoing source of data on AOD use and its consequences from several large, methodologically sound surveys conducted by various federal agencies. Youth, adults, arrestees, and AOD involvement in hospital emergency room visits are subject to regular, large, and methodologically sound surveys. The major US surveys on AOD use include the following.

National Survey on Drug Use (NSDUH)

The National Survey on Drug Use and Health (NSDUH) has been conducted since 1971 (Substance Abuse and Mental Health Services Administration, 2010). In 2009, 68,700 civilian, non-institutionalised individuals answered questions about their drug use via computer in their homes. Participants were 12 or older, with the upper boundary set at 65 or older. There was a 75.7% completion rate.

National Epidemiologic Survey on Alcohol and Related Conditions (NESARC)

The NESARC was a national survey conducted in 2001–2 and repeated in 2004–5 (National Institute on Alcohol Abuse and Alcoholism, 2006). The survey measured alcohol consumption and alcohol use disorders, five mood disorders, four anxiety disorders, seven personality disorders, illicit drug use and disorders, tobacco use, and alcohol treatment. A total of 43,093 participants 18 years old and older were interviewed in their homes. Overall there was an 81% response rate. Sampling was complex, dividing the USA into geographical regions, randomly sampling within these regions, but oversampling blacks and Hispanics to be sure that representative samples of these groups were large enough. Then when data were calculated, weighting formulas were applied to appropriately reflect the US population. The 3-year follow- up comprised 34,653 of the original 43,093 participants, a 70.2% response rate.

Arrestee Drug Abuse Monitoring Program (ADAMII)

This study is conducted in 10 US counties. Participants are interviewed within 48 hours of arrest (Office of National Drug Control Policy, Executive Office of the President, 2009). The sample consists of all male arrestees during two 2-week periods in each of the 10 counties. In 2008, 4,592 booked arrestees were interviewed and 3,924 gave urine specimens. The interview lasts for 20–25 minutes, after which a urine sample is requested, which is tested for 10 drugs. The interview is voluntary, with a 60% response rate. Of those interviewed, 86% provided a urine sample.

The Drug Abuse Warning Network (DAWN)

The DAWN project estimates the number of drug-related emergency department (ED) visits each year (Substance Abuse and Mental Health Services Administration, Center for Behavioral Health

Statistics and Quality, 2011). All types of drugs are included: legal, illegal, alcohol, and medications. In 2008, 231 hospitals in 13 metropolitan areas participated. Patient charts are reviewed for ED visits that are drug related. Data are weighted (corrected) to best reflect overall ED trends in the USA.

Monitoring the future (MTF)

The Monitoring the Future study (Johnston et al., 2011) examines drug use in 8th, 10th, 12th grade and college each year. In 2010, over 46,000 students participated. The research is carefully conducted to gain information reflecting the overall trends in use among adolescents. In order to select a representative group of students, geographic areas are chosen and then schools are chosen within these regions. Students are randomly chosen within the school to fill out a questionnaire on their drug use.

Recent trends in drug use

In this section, I focus on four important recent trends in drug use patterns: the extensive use of both marijuana and non-medical use of prescription drugs, the high rate of drug use among arrestees, and the dramatic reduction in cigarette smoking. For now, I just mention the epidemiological findings; later I will discuss the implications.

In 2009, the NSDUH estimated that 6.6% of US citizens 12 or older use marijuana at least monthly and 1.7% had a marijuana use disorder (Substance Abuse and Mental Health Services Administration, 2010). Over 6% of 12th graders reported using marijuana daily and over 21% used it at least monthly in 2010 (Johnston et al., 2011). Certainly these statistics are cause for concern and suggest current policies for prevention are not effective.

Non-medical use of prescription drugs is the next largest type of illicit drug use: 2.8% of NSDUH respondents reported such use in the past month; 8% of 12 graders report the non-medical use of pain killers in the past year. While the rate has remained at this level for the last decade, little has been done to address this problem.

Among arrestees interviewed in ADAM II, 87% tested positive for drugs. Arrestees use drugs much more frequently than the general population, typically several times a month (Office of National Drug Control Policy, Executive Office of the President, 2009). About half of the US incarcerated population has a substance use disorder (SUD) (National Center on Addiction and Substance Abuse at Columbia, 2010). Most of these offenders do not receive substance abuse treatment and a large percentage go on to reoffend.

Cigarette consumption has decreased in the past decade. According to the NSDUH survey, 30.4% of those 12 or older smoked in the past month in 2002. The number has steadily decreased since then to 27.7% in 2009. This success story has largely been ignored but it has implications for understanding the nature of addiction and implications for policy.

Substance abuse treatment in the USA

The substance abuse system in the USA has remained largely the same for the past 30 years, still separate, as a rule, from the mental health system (Miller et al., 2006). Community substance abuse treatment programmes are licensed by the states. These programmes are staffed mostly by substance abuse counsellors (McLellan & Meyers, 2004). Their education and training is modest. Counsellors who are accredited or licensed have generally 400 hours of education that is specific to substance abuse counselling and a supervised internship of one year. However, a fairly large percentage of the staff have no such substance abuse credential or licence. In a survey of counsellors working in model programmes, only 63% were certified or licensed (Rieckmann et al.,

2011). Psychosocial treatments predominate including 12-step facilitation, cognitive behavioural therapy (CBT), and some motivational interviewing (MI). For drug abuse, therapeutic community and outpatient drug treatment are available. For opiate addiction, methadone maintenance programmes (MMTP) are offered. Brief descriptions of these treatments are given below. Most treatment is offered on an outpatient basis.

There is an increasingly greater interface between substance abuse treatment and the criminal justice system because of the high rate of SUD (substance use disorder) among the offender population. Drug courts have become popular that divert low-level offenders from incarceration into treatment (Mitchell, 2012). In prison, treatment is provided to offenders with SUD. Still, only a small fraction of offenders with SUD receive any substantial treatment (Welsh, 2007). In addition to increasing the capacity, substance abuse treatment needs to be tailored to the special needs of this population, many of whom have comorbid mental disorders (National Center on Addiction and Substance Abuse at Columbia, 2010).

Because of the separation of the mental health and substance abuse treatment systems in the USA, treatment for those with a comorbid mental disorder and SUD has been problematic. Since clients with both disorders do not respond well to conventional substance abuse treatment (Drake et al. 1993, 1998), treatment for this population must be greatly modified from standard substance abuse treatment. For over a decade, efforts have been made to increase the availability of integrated treatment, designed specifically for those with comorbid disorders. It provides comprehensive treatment for both disorders in the same facility on an inpatient or outpatient basis. However, there are not nearly enough of these programmes.

Common treatment modalities and some promising ESIs

The common treatment modalities for drug abuse in the USA are the therapeutic community, methadone maintenance treatment and outpatient drug treatment.

MMTP

This is an opioid replacement therapy. Clients take an oral dose of methadone daily to reduce or eliminate the craving for heroin (Hubbard et al., 1989). Depending on the programme, there may be some substance abuse counselling in conjunction with the administration of methadone.

Therapeutic community

The TC is an inpatient programme lasting from 6 to 12 months. TC treatment elements include: encounter groups, peer counselling groups, seminars (psycho-education), rewards and punishments, assigned job functions, and ex-addict and ex-felon staff role models (Nielsen & Scarpitti, 1997; Wexler & Williams, 1986).

Drug-free outpatient substance abuse programmes

These outpatient programmes use counselling as their primary intervention rather than medication. These programmes are less structured than the others and may focus on complete change or essentially consist of crisis management. There is great heterogeneity among these programmes in staffing, treatment philosophy, and implementation (Hubbard et al., 1989). The common treatment modalities for alcoholism treatment are 12-step facilitation, cognitive behavioural therapy, and motivational interviewing.

Twelve-step facilitation model (TSF)

This professional treatment has been called the Minnesota Model, the Disease Concept, and 12-step treatment. The treatment is based on the premise that active participation in Alcoholics Anonymous (AA) will help the alcoholic become and remain sober. Thus the primary goal is to promote AA involvement. Techniques include education about alcoholism and helping the patient confront the effects of his drinking on his life. The counsellor teaches practical methods of staying sober based on the experiences of AA members. TSF is the predominant type of alcoholism treatment provided in the USA.

Cognitive behavioural treatment (CBT)

This treatment for alcohol disorders is based on the view that excessive drinking is a learned habit. The treatment consists of employing methods to unlearn the maladaptive drinking behaviours and thought patterns and teach adaptive skills regarding the drinking behaviour and general life skills. There are several types of CBT including relapse prevention. Each type of CBT contains a combination of didactic topics, which may include training in drink refusal skills, coping with alcohol environments, problem solving, interpersonal skills, mood regulation, coping skills for dealing with stress, communication skills and assertiveness training.

Motivational interviewing (MI)

This type of treatment has as its goal the development of motivation for the individual to change the addictive behaviour (Miller & Rollnick, 1991, 2002). Since most clients enter treatment with little motivation to change, MI views building motivation of primary importance, especially at the beginning of treatment. Instead of focusing on drinking behaviour, the counsellor focuses on the client's ambivalence or lack thereof regarding the drinking. The goal is to create ambivalence when there is none, and when there is, help the client resolve it on the side of quitting. The techniques are based in part on client-centred therapy such as empathic listening to engage the patient's cooperation.

ESIs and models of substance abuse treatment

Additionally, there are some promising ESIs and two new treatment models for substance abuse treatment in the USA.

Contingency management

Contingency management (sometimes called motivational incentives or voucher programmes) offers incentives or rewards to encourage specific behavioural goals. In the case of treatment for substance dependence, monetary and non-monetary rewards typically have been made contingent on attendance and negative toxicology screens, indicating abstinence from drug use (Dutra et al., 2008).

Community reinforcement approach (CRA)

CRA uses family, social, recreational and occupational rewards to move the client towards abstinence so that a clean and sober lifestyle is more rewarding than one with AOD. Various types of skills training are included. Significant others are involved in treatment whenever possible (Smith et al., 2001).

Buprenorphine

Buprenorphine is a drug that has been found to reduce the craving for heroin. Like methadone, it is an opioid replacement therapy but it has a safer drug profile than methadone. Unlike methadone, which may be dispensed only in licensed methadone clinics in the USA, this may be dispensed by physicians who are certified addiction specialists (members of the American Society of Addiction Medicine) or physicians who have received specific buprenorphine training.

Behavioural couples therapy

Behavioural couples therapy is a highly structured programme of 15–20 sessions delivered over 5 to 6 months (Fals-Stewart, O'Farrell, & Birchler, 2004). The goals of the therapy are to eliminate unsafe AOD use usually through abstinence, to engage the family's support for the patient's effort to change, and to improve couple and family interaction, which will, in turn, promote long-term abstinence.

Additionally, there are two new models of US substance abuse treatment: the stepped care model (Scott & Dennis, 2011) and recovery management (Hser & Anglin, 2011), both of which are based on seeing substance use disorders as a chronic illness. These approaches are still in the early stages of development.

The concept of continuing care

Continuing care can be seen as an effort to respond to the chronic nature of SUD. If clients are not attending or achieving their objectives in primary treatment, continuing care elements can monitor this and provide intervention as needed, such as home visits, telephone contacts, or referral for more intensive treatment (Scott & Dennis, 2011). For the most part, however, continuing care occurs after the intensive initial treatment is completed (McKay, 2009). It can include group counselling, individual therapy, case management, telephone counselling, brief checkups, couples therapy, family participation, home visits, and self-help meetings and special self-help facilitation and coordination.

Recovery management

Recently, SAMSHA has endorsed the concept of recovery management (Hser & Anglin, 2011). The concept is not fully fleshed out but incorporates the idea of continuing care. It has provision for recovery coaches, recovery support specialists, and community recovery support centres, all of which have yet to be clearly defined. But the intention is to incorporate those who have recovered from SUD to be a part of the treatment system beyond the current ad hoc situation where many substance abuse counsellors are in recovery. How this will be integrated into current treatment is not yet worked out.

Outcome research on substance abuse treatment

A great deal of research on substance abuse treatment outcome has been conducted. In some respects, there is good news. On the plus side, an extensive research literature shows that US substance abuse treatment as currently delivered reduces drug use, increases rates of abstinence, and this effect lasts for several years compared to no treatment (Berglund et al., 2003; Hubbard et al., 2003; Miller et al., 2001). Still, the improvement while significantly higher than no treatment, is not spectacular. On the negative side, it is found that clients drop out of treatment at high rates (Carroll et al., 2011; Dutra et al., 2008) and most of those who stay in treatment are not fully treatment compliant (i.e., miss many scheduled sessions) (Carroll et al., 2011).

The research on ESIs shows that specific ESIs have an advantage over treatment as usual (TAU) but not other ESIs (Carroll & Rounsaville, 2007). For example, while cognitive behavioural therapy (CBT) and motivational interviewing (MI) outcomes are better than TAU, MI outcomes are not better than CBT and vice versa. The most promising ESIs, behavioural couples therapy, contingency management, and the community reinforcement a approach have not been widely adopted by community treatment programmes.

A challenge for community programmes is to determine which ESIs to adopt. Given that NREPP lists 80 ESIs for substance abuse (Substance Abuse and Mental Health Services Administration, 2013) and no ESI has shown to be superior, on what basis should programmes decide which ESI to use? In terms of education and training, how can we decide which approaches to teach? It is not possible to teach them all. One approach would be to teach ESI principles rather than specific interventions (Carroll & Rounsaville, 2007).

Help outside the treatment system

In addition to the formal treatment system, there is now a growing outcome research literature on other approaches to help those with AOD problems. These include brief interventions, telephone hotlines, self-help groups (especially AA), and natural recovery.

Brief interventions lasting from 3 to 15 minutes conducted by physicians and other medical professionals have shown to reduce hazardous drinking (Kaner, 2007; Salaspuro, 2003; Whitlock et al., 2004) and increase successful quitting of smoking (Clinical Practice Guideline, 2008). Telephone quit lines are also somewhat helpful for smoking cessation (Brandon et al., 2009).

Sobell (2007) has summarised the findings of natural recovery from AOD. She notes that the majority of people who reduce or stop their drinking, smoking, and even use of drugs do so on their own without formal help. The stability of these recoveries is good, with follow-ups lasting 6–8 years. Floter and Kroger (2007) note that between 70–85% of smokers who successfully quit stop without help. However, they typically require 14 and 15 attempts before they are successful. (To be fair, it should be noted that when clients use nicotine replacement medications they are more likely to successfully quit than those who do not [Brandon et. al. 2009].)

In the past decade, a great deal of research has been conducted on the effectiveness of AA. The research provides good evidence that AA is effective in helping those with alcohol use disorders to become abstinent and improve in other areas of their lives (Humphreys et al., 2004). It is somewhat ironic that this approach, which is based on convictions that are not supported by research, should turn out to be so effective and in some respects superior to conventional treatment. The success of AA can be seen as support for the chronic disease model as well as support for help outside the treatment system. On the one hand, the core conviction of AA, that alcoholism is an incurable disease, clearly puts it in the chronic disease camp as well as the long-term commitment AA members make to remain active in AA. On the other hand, since AA is a self-help group with no professional involvement, it could be argued it is not like the professional chronic medical disease model of treatment.

Emerging trends in treatment

Thus, there are two emerging divergent trends in dealing with those with substance problems in the USA. One trend is the chronic disease model, which is intended for those who have substance use disorders that will need ongoing care at various levels for an indefinite period. The stepped care model is based on this concept. A minimal intervention approach is the other trend, which includes natural recovery, brief intervention, and self-help. While it is tempting to say that those with mild problems should fare better in the light intervention condition and those with severe problems would fare better in the chronic model, the case of tobacco dependence makes that difficult to maintain. First, tobacco is one of the most addictive substances. Despite this, in the past decade hundreds of thousands of smokers have quit. Most who have quit did so on their own even though most had to try 14 or 15 times before they were successful. These ex-smokers demonstrate that while difficult, the task of confronting an addiction can be done with little or no external help. So a critical question remains: who are good candidates for which overall approach? Another concern is that the informal system of brief intervention, helplines, natural recovery is not linked to the professional treatment system.

The stepped care model can be seen as bridging the two trends. Thus, clients who do not respond to a mild or moderate intervention can be provided more intensive care, thus bridging both the chronic and brief intervention models. Another advantage of the stepped care model is that clients who are doing well can be stepped down from treatment intensity while those having trouble can have their intensity increased. The stepped care model is also philosophically aligned with connecting the informal and formal treatment systems.

Prevention issues

From longitudinal research, childhood risk and protective factors for AOD problems have been identified: behavioural undercontrol, which includes externalising problems, problem behaviour, poor adjustment and coping, and aggressive behaviour in childhood and adolescence are linked to later AOD problems (Zucker, 2008). Family factors can also increase the risk for later AOD problems. Parents who are inattentive (Hayatbakhsh et al., 2008), provide poor discipline (Pears et al., 2007), use AOD (Ryan et al., 2010), and stress in the family (Alati et al., 2010) are all risk factors for later AOD problems in their children. Protective factors come from parents who are supportive, have good relationships with their children, monitor their children, and disapprove of drinking (Ryan, 2010). The following types of intervention are based on these research findings and thus can be considered ESIs.

Parent education programmes focus on developing a positive bond between the mother and infant and meeting the child's developmental needs (Toumbourou, Williams, and Patton 2005). Parents of older children are taught parenting skills. Family intervention programmes have also been developed to help at-risk families. Pilot programmes in some substance abuse treatment programmes have provided parent education to their clients who are parents (Haggerty et al., 2008).

Another prevention approach is to target those children with behaviorual problems with interventions so they will be more capable of doing well in school and less likely to resort to AOD (Stockwell et al., 2005). One such approach is to enhance the school environment to teach these and all children to develop good behavioural control (Kellam et al., 2011).

While the focus of this paper is on drugs and alcohol, the longitudinal research suggests that prevention efforts to reduce behavioural undercontrol could result in reductions of many negative outcomes in addition to AOD problems: truancy, delinquency, mental disorders, early pregnancy, risky sexual behaviours, violence, and early school dropouts (Stockwell et al., 2005).

Drug and alcohol education programmes for high school students vary in their effectiveness (Elliot et al., 2005). Information programmes, fear tactics, focus on self-esteem, reduce peer pressure or advice not to drink until the legal age have proved ineffective.

Other interventions discussed in other sections of this chapter can also be considered aspects of prevention: screening and brief intervention, restricting sale of legal drugs such as increased taxes on tobacco. Prevention could also address the relationship between AOD, risky sex, and violence including those in substance abuse treatment.

Effective and ineffective governmental drug policy

Current US policy on psychoactive drugs has two distinct philosophies. On the one hand, drugs deemed addictive, harmful and without medical value are prohibited. On the other, alcohol and tobacco are legal but are subject to government regulation. In between are drugs with medical value that, nevertheless, have addictive potential. These drugs, including opiate pain killers can be legally prescribed, but their distribution is more restricted than typical prescription drugs.

While there is little secret that the policy of prohibiting drugs has been a failure (Robinson, 2007), it is less commonly known that restricting the availability of tobacco (Chaloupka, 2010) and alcohol (Babor, 2010) has been an effective policy. These restrictions have not eliminated all harms but they have been shown to significantly reduce them. The simplest and most logical approach has been shown to have the greatest impact: simply raising the price of tobacco and alcohol has reduced consumption and hazards associated with their use. This policy could even have a greater positive impact by raising the tax on alcohol, which on an inflation-adjusted basis, is 37% lower now than it was in 1991(Marr & Brunet, 2009). For alcohol, other restrictions such as reducing alcohol sales in neighbourhoods, better DWI enforcement, lowering the BAC for DWI, zero tolerance laws, which provide sanctions for drivers under 21 with any BAC above .00, and the minimum legal drinking age have all shown significant and positive effects. Better enforcement would have an even greater impact.

This is minor tweaking compared to the problems with the war on drugs, which by all accounts has been a failure. The tension between states that permit medical marijuana and recreational use of marijuana and the federal government that classifies marijuana as a schedule I drug must be resolved. Can marijuana be safely regulated in a manner similar to alcohol and tobacco? This debate is front and centre; research at this point can only say that marijuana should not be considered a schedule I drug. One might infer from this that regulation may be effective for marijuana as it has been for tobacco and alcohol. Contrariwise, there are risks associated with allowing any psychoactive drug to become more available.

But very much under the radar is prescription drug abuse. One reason for this may simply be that these drugs are not black or white: they serve a useful function but can be highly addictive. Three efforts to deal with the problem are mentioned in the literature: prescription drug-monitoring programmes funded by the office of national drug control policy (Fornili & Simoni-Wastila, 2011), better education of physicians to be alert to misuse of psychoactive drugs (Smith, 2012) and attention to physicians who may be overprescribing (Ziegler, Goldenbaum, & Donald, 2011). There is no research to show whether these approaches are helpful. It is not clear how requisite quantities of these drugs are diverted and how many are simply taken from medicine cabinets of unused prescriptions, or what percentage of patients who had been prescribed these drugs become addicted. This is an area of addiction in which more research is warranted. As a first step to intervene it would make sense to develop a programme to educate patients about their medications, advising them to dispose of unused psychoactive medications, and provide rebates for doing so.

The research process: research, translation, dissemination, and improvement of the treatment system

Currently SAMSHA, NIDA, and NIAA are advocating ESIs through SAMSHA's NREPP initiative. But states do not have to follow this recommendation. For over 30 years, researchers, notably Bill Miller (Miller et al., 2006), have complained that treatment programmes do not adopt ESIs. This is still the case (Tai et al., 2010) and there is no sign it is likely to change. In fact, the state authorities that regulate substance abuse treatment have much more basic problems to contend with. Community programmes are burdened with large paperwork requirements, multiple regulatory bodies to report to, insufficient revenue stream, high rates of staff turnover (McLellan, Carise, & Kleber, 2003; Rieckmann et al., 2011) and insufficient supervisory staff (Amodeo, Storti, & Larson, 2010). Amodeo et al. (2006) in their effort to implement ESIs in two community clinics found that the clinics had many deficiencies of standard practice, including ethics violations. They note that before ESIs can be successfully implemented in programmes, basic good counselling practices must be firmly in place.

Neither is the workforce is not well trained. In their limited training, counsellors are not introduced in a systematic way to the current research or how to understand it in contrast to most other mental health professionals. As a consequence, counsellors are not trained to understand or implement ESIs. A good case example of the difficulty in getting substance abuse counsellors to accept research findings is methadone maintenance treatment programs (MMTP). While outcome research consistently shows good outcomes for MMTP, many in the counselling profession discount these findings (Fitzgerald & McCarty, 2009) with anecdotal evidence of misuse of the drug, its failure in specific cases, and their informal observation of local methadone clinics.

Perhaps the most sobering way of looking at the issue is that no matter what approach is taken to translation and diffusion of new interventions, the current treatment system as currently constituted cannot absorb it in any meaningful way.

How successful have Community Trials Network (CTN) and addiction technology transfer centers (ATTC) been?

Community Trials Network (CTN)

Established in 1999 (Tai et al., 2010), the CTN created a network of community-based treatment research centres, which investigates the effectiveness of ESIs in 240 affiliated community-based programmes (Martino et al., 2010), including motivational incentives (contingency management) and buprenorphine. The CTN has completed 27 treatment studies comprising 13,000 subjects (Nunes, 2011). It has also fostered the dissemination and implementation of ESIs in community programmes. Their results show that CTN community programmes are more open to ESIs (Ducharme et al., 2010) and more likely to adopt them (Martino et al., 2010) than typical community programmes. One of the important findings of the CTNs is that the process of a programme adopting an ESI is not easy. It involves not only training and education but coaching and feedback provided in close supervision (Miller et al., 2006). As indicated above, most community programmes do not have the resources to provide enough coaching, feedback, and supervision (Carroll & Rounsaville, 2007). CTN researchers have also investigated barriers to implementation by surveying administrators and members of the addiction treatment workforce. Roman et al. (2010) found that many substance abuse counsellors and programmes had treatment ideologies that were inconsistent with either medications such as buprenorphine or contingency management, both of which are well-supported ESIs. In addition, many counsellors do not accept the scientific evidence supporting these ESIs or believe that the evidence is inadequate. Amodeo et al. (2010) note that clinical staff often work autonomously using treatment practices they prefer and resist new practices.

Addiction technology transfer centers (ATTCS)

The 14 regional ATTCs' mission is to implement evidence-based practices in substance abuse treatment. They publish papers, periodicals, curricula, videos, and make presentations as well as provide training to foster implementation of ESIs (Martino et al., 2010).

Blending initiatives were begun in 2001 that combine the research experience of CTN with efforts by ATTCs to disseminate the results (Martino et al., 2010). They have created initiatives for buprenorphine, motivational incentives (contingency management), and motivational interviewing among others. From 2007 to 2012, there were 63,283 downloads of blending products and 2,432 trainings on ESIs given (Stephanie Richards, 2013, personal communication). There has been no research on the effectiveness of the products or training, however.

Currently, there is no information on the impact of the ATTCS or CTNs on the adoption of ESIs in community programmes. In regard to changing the community substance abuse treatment system, while not absolutely proved, it is fairly clear that the CTNs and ATTCs have not markedly improved the adoption of ESIs. McGovern et al. (2013) estimate that about 25% of community programmes use some ESIs. There have been some important lessons learned, however. Among the most important is that adoption of ESIs is difficult to achieve and maintained. But the most substantial factor is the disconnect between the SAMSHA's goal of instituting ESIs and the state of community substance abuse facilities. Most treatment programmes simply do not have adequate resources to incorporate ESIs. In many cases, they are not able to provide adequate standard care. To make an analogy, an innovative educational elementary school programme will not work if the schools are not safe, organised, and the teachers not sufficiently skilled no matter how good the innovation.

Perhaps the only constructive suggestion that can be made in regard to ESIs is for SAMSHA to focus on substance abuse counsellor education. Neither the CTN nor the ATTCs have made this a significant focus of their efforts. If counsellors receive better training that includes an introduction to understanding research, they would be more likely to be open to it. However, on a more basic level, it appears that the most important consideration should be raising the level of care to a reasonable standard in community substance abuse programmes. This would include better counselling training, sufficient staffing, and sufficient supervision. It means finding ways to reduce the rapid staff turnover in many programs. From my analysis, it appears that adoption of ESIs is not a feasible goal in community programmes at this time. If this analysis is correct, it could be concluded that CTN and ATTCs have an idealistic mission that is unrealistic given the state of the current substance abuse treatment system.

Back to the drawing board

Looking at the treatment system and process treatment research, it makes sense to consider conducting research that examines the state of the substance abuse treatment system. If I am right along with others such as McLellan and Amodeo, it would be better to reconfigure the treatment system so that basic services can be provided in a professional and ethical manner. Additionally, it makes sense to conduct research on what counsellors actually do and why they do it as well as assessing the needs of the clients they treat. This could be important since Santa Ana et al. (2008) suggest that counsellors stated orientation may not reflect what they actually do in sessions. A related type of research is process research, which focuses on what goes on in treatment (Hubble, Duncan, and Miller, 1999). Such research can investigate what elements of treatment bring about positive change and can find practices that may be independent of the differing treatment models. Current outcome research has not given programmes clear direction since there are no ESIs that are better than other ESIs. Process research may provide much better direction to community programmes in determining what will work best in their settings. To date a good deal of process research has focused on the early therapeutic relationship between counsellor and client. Meier et al. (2005) reviewed the research on the effect of treatment alliance in substance abuse treatment. Therapeutic alliances measured early in drug treatment predict greater retention and engagement in treatment and reduced criminal activity. Another example of process research with practical implications is the finding that more directiveness on the part of counsellors has led to more resistance in clients (Karno & Longabaugh, 2005). With information like this in hand, realistic modifications can be proposed that move in the direction of better practice in community programmes.

The wealth of information relevant to substance abuse

As stated earlier, I have just completed a text on substance abuse research. I have read literally thousands of research articles, reviews, and meta-analyses on substance abuse. In my extensive review, I found some exemplary research projects, some excellent reviews, a great deal of duplication, and a few gems. Sometimes I found the same conclusion in different review articles with completely different citations as well as different conclusions drawn from the same citations!

What should be done to improve the translation of research into practice? Since the 1990s, NIDA and other federal agencies have committed a great deal of time and effort into bringing research into the community substance abuse system (Brown & Flynn, 2002). Yet, this has not resulted in any large-scale change in behaviour or attitude. Interested clinicians are looking into a very tangled jungle to find coherent useful findings. Of course, the main goal of our book is to make relevant research findings accessible to clinicians. But realistically, the book will not become a best seller. Much more time should be spent digesting the voluminous research. One idea is that reviewer and synthesiser of research become a recognised role. Publications dedicated to summarising and distilling research findings should be developed.

For the past 30 years, treatment research has largely focused on what type of treatment has the best outcomes. The results show that any ESI treatment is better than TAU; but no ESI is better than any other ESI, making it difficult for programmes to determine which ESI to adopt. Efforts to infuse ESIs into community programmes have proved difficult. Some researchers argue that additional research needs to be conducted to determine the best methods to infuse ESIs into community programmes (McGovern et al., 2013). My analysis suggests that this approach would not markedly change the community substance abuse system because it is burdened with many issues that make it difficult for them to provide even a reasonable level of care. Are there better ways to determine what to research and how to research it? I suggest that research on the current treatment system, process research, and research on the needs of the clients in the treatment system would provide more useful knowledge. For example, a large number of substance abuse patients have comorbid psychiatric conditions yet there have been no ESIs developed to address special considerations for their successful treatment. Thus, to reiterate, I believe a good investment would be to research actual treatment practices and clients in addiction treatment programmes and to focus on treatment processes rather than ESIs or implementation research. This knowledge I believe would be more relevant and more easily adapted to the current treatment system.

Overall recommendations

Policy

The war on drugs has been by all accounts a failure. What is not so clear is what should replace it. Given the conflict between the federal prohibitionist policy on marijuana and the states that have sanctioned medical and recreational use of marijuana, a good place to start would be to develop a new policy regarding marijuana. Regarding alcohol and tobacco policy, research is clear that raising the price and other restrictions on these legal drugs has been successful. Higher prices through raising taxes and other restrictions on alcohol and tobacco should be implemented.

Treatment

The substance abuse system remains separated from the mental health system in the United States. The substance abuse system does not have the expertise to provide appropriate care for the large number of clients with comorbid mental disorders. By the same token, the mental health system does not have in place expertise to help their mental health clients with substance use disorders. Integrated treatment (IT) is a model of treatment that intervenes to help clients with both disorders but has not been adopted on any large scale. A much greater focus needs to be placed on treatment for this population, including more refinement and research on IT. Community substance abuse treatment has not changed in the past 30 years. Efforts by SAMSHA to bring ESIs into these programmes on any large scale have not succeeded. My analysis suggests that this is not a feasible goal because the current treatment system does not have the capacity to absorb new treatment modalities. It lacks the resources to do so, including adequate staffing, supervision, and organisation. A more realistic goal at this time would be to raise the level of care in community programmes to acceptable standards of care.

Recently, the view that addictive disorders are chronic medical conditions that warrant continuing care has been put forward (McLellan et al., 2000). This is certainly true for a percentage of those with SUD. For these individuals, such a model makes sense. The continuing care model of treatment fits the conception of addictive disorders as a chronic illness. Another current but diverging trend is to provide minimal interventions to help those with addictive disorders. These interventions include screening and brief interventions, telephone hotlines, self-help, and natural recovery. The stepped care model appears to be a potential bridge between these two approaches.

Prevention

A rich source of knowledge about child and adolescent development has been amassed by longitudinal studies. These studies have identified risk and protective factors for the development of SUDs. Prevention programmes have been developed that are based on these findings. These programmes work to help children develop more behavioural control in school or at home through parent education. Some target at-risk populations. While showing a great deal of promise, they have not been adopted on a large scale.

Addiction education for mental health professionals

First and foremost substance abuse counsellor education needs improvement. Attention to basic counselling skills, ethics, and addiction knowledge should be included in curricula. Introduction to basic research methods and respect for their results should be included. Support should be given to the International Coalition for Addiction Studies Education (INCASE), which is the professional organisation for educators in addiction studies. In partnership with the professional substance abuse counsellors association (NAADAC) and others, INCASE has created the National Addiction Studies Accreditation Commission. Additionally, all mental health professionals should have sufficient education about addiction.

Research and dissemination

There is an immense body of research on substance use and abuse. The USA has a rich ongoing source of data on AOD use and its consequences from several large, methodologically sound surveys conducted by various federal agencies. Longitudinal studies have provided valuable information about the risk factors and course of addictive disorders. There is an extensive body of research on treatment outcome. Unfortunately, this knowledge has not filtered down into treatment programmes. Efforts by SAMSHA through the CTN and ATTCs have not appreciably helped. I suggest that research into what programmes are actually doing and developing more modest goals for these programmes is a more realistic path to pursue at this time.

I have suggested that more attention be paid to organising, distilling, and integrating the great body of research become a focus for the field. This could include a group of specialists whose main focus would be to provide this integration. It would also include publications that would give clinicians useful findings from the research for their clinical work in a useful format.

References

Alati, R., Maloney, E., Hutchinson, D. M., Najman, J. M., Mattick, R. P., Bor, W. et al. (2010). Do maternal parenting practices predict problematic patterns of adolescent alcohol consumption? *Addiction, 105*(5), 872–880.

Amodeo, M., Ellis, M. A., & Samet, J. H. (2006). Introducing evidence-based practices into substance abuse treatment using organization development methods. *American Journal of Drug and Alcohol Abuse, 32*(4), 555–560.

Amodeo, M., Storti, S. A., & Larson, M. J. (2010). Moving empirically supported practices to addiction treatment programs: Recruiting supervisors to help in technology transfer. *Substance Use & Misuse, 45*(6), 968–982.

Babor, T. (2010). *Alcohol: No ordinary commodity: Research and public policy.* Oxford and New York: Oxford University Press.

Berglund, M., Thelander, S., & Jonsson, E. (2003). In M. Berglund, S. Thelander, & E. Jonsson (Eds.), *Treating alcohol and drug abuse: An evidence based review.* Weinheim: Wiley-VCH Verlag GmbH & Co. KGaA.

Brandon, T. H., Drobes, D. J., Ditre, J. W., & Elibero, A. (2009). In L. M. Cohen, F. L. Collins, A. M. Young, D. E. McChargue, T. R. Leffingwell, & K. L. Cook (Eds.), *Nicotine.* New York, NY: Routledge/Taylor & Francis Group.

Brown, B. S., & Flynn, P. M. (2002). The federal role in drug abuse technology transfer: A history and perspective. *Journal of Substance Abuse Treatment, 22*(4), 244–257.

Carroll, K. M., Ball, S. A., Jackson, R., Martino, S., Petry, N. M., Stitzer, M. L. et al. (2011). Ten take home lessons from the first 10 years of the CTN and 10 recommendations for the future. *American Journal of Drug and Alcohol Abuse, 37*(5), 275–282.

Carroll, K. M., & Rounsaville, B. J. (2007). A vision of the next generation of behavioral therapies research in the addictions. *Addiction, 102*(6), 850–862.

Chaloupka, F. (2010). Tobacco control lessons learned: The impact of state and local policies. ImpacTeen. http://www.impacteen.org/generalarea_PDFs/ ITResearch38_Chaloupka.pdf (accessed 29 August 2012).

Clinical Practice Guideline for Treating Tobacco Use and Dependence. (2008). 2008 update on a U.S. public health service report. *American Journal of Preventive Medicine, 35*(2), 158–176.

Drake, R. E. Bartels, S. J., Teague, G. B., Noordsy, D. L., & Clark, R. E. (1993). Treatment of substance abuse in severely mentally ill patients. *Journal of Nervous and Mental Disease*, 181, 606–611.

Drake, R. E., Mercer-McFadden, C., Mueser, K. T., McHugo, G. J., & Bond, G. R. (1998). Review of integrated mental health and substance abuse treatment for patients with dual disorders. *Schizophrenia Bulletin*, 24, 589–608.

Ducharme, L. J., Knudsen, H. K., Abraham, A. J., & Roman, P. M. (2010). Counselor attitudes toward the use of motivational incentives in addiction treatment. *American Journal on Addictions, 19*(6), 496–503.

Dutra, L., Stathopoulou, G., Basden, S. L., Leyro, T. M., Powers, M. B., & Otto, M. W. (2008). A meta-analytic review of psychosocial interventions for substance use disorders. *American Journal of Psychiatry, 165*(2), 179–187.

Elliott, L., Orr, L., Watson, L., & Jackson, A. (2005). Secondary prevention interventions for young drug users: A systematic review of the evidence. *Adolescence, 40*(157), 1–22.

Fals-Stewart, W., O'Farrell, T. J., Birchler, G. R. (2004). Behavioral couples therapy for substance abuse: Rationale, methods, and findings. *Science and Practice Perspectives*, 2, 30–41.

Fitzgerald, J., & McCarty, D. (2009). Understanding attitudes toward use of medication in substance abuse treatment: A multilevel approach. *Psychological Services, 6*(1), 74–84.

Floter, S., & Kroger, C. (2007). Self-change: The rule among smokers. In H. Klingermann & L. C. Sobell (Eds.), *Promoting self-change from addictive behavior: Practical implications for policy, prevention, and treatment* (pp. 105–111). New York: Springer.
Fornili, K., & Simoni-Wastila, L. (2011). Prescription monitoring programs: Striking the balance between medical use and diversion. *Journal of Addictions Nursing, 22*(1–2), 77–82.
Haggerty, K. P., Skinner, M., Fleming, C. B., Gainey, R. R., & Catalano, R. F. (2008). Long-term effects of the focus on families project on substance use disorders among children of parents in methadone treatment. *Addiction, 103*(12), 2008–2016.
Hayatbakhsh, M. R., Mamun, A. A., Najman, J. M., O'Callaghan, M. J., Bor, W., & Alati, R. (2008). Early childhood predictors of early substance use and substance use disorders: Prospective study. *Australian and New Zealand Journal of Psychiatry, 42*(8), 720–731.
Hser, Y., & Anglin, M. D. (2011). Addiction treatment and recovery careers. In J. F. Kelly & W. L. White (Eds.), *Addiction recovery management: Theory, research, and practice* (pp. 9–29). Totowa, NJ: Humana Press.
Hubbard, R. L., Craddock, S. G., & Anderson, J. (2003). Overview of 5-year followup outcomes in the drug abuse treatment outcome studies (DATOS). *Journal of Substance Abuse Treatment, 25*(3), 125–134.
Hubbard, R. L., Marsden, M. E., Rachal, J. V., Harwood, H. J., Cavanaugh, E. R., & Ginzburg, H. M. (1989). *Drug abuse treatment: A national study of effectiveness*. Chapel Hill, NC: University of North Carolina Press.
Hubble, M. A., Duncan, B. L., and Miller, S. D. (1999). *The heart and soul of change: What works in therapy*. Washington, DC: American Psychological Association.
Humphreys, K., Wing, S., McCarty, D., Chappel, J., Gallant, L., Haberle, B. et al. (2004). Self-help organizations for alcohol and drug problems: Toward evidence-based practice and policy. *Journal of Substance Abuse Treatment, 26*(3), 151–158.
Johnston, L. D., O'Malley, P. M., Bachman, J. G., & Schulenberg, J. E. (2011). *Monitoring the Future national results on adolescent drug use: Overview of key findings, 2010*. Ann Arbor, MI: Institute for Social Research, University of Michigan.
Kaner, E. F. (2007). Effectiveness of brief alcohol interventions in primary care populations. *Cochrane Database Systematic Review*, 18 April, (2) CD004148.
Karno, M. P., & Longabaugh, R. (2005). Less directiveness by therapists improves drinking outcomes of reactant clients in alcoholism treatment. *Journal of Consulting and Clinical Psychology, 73*(2), 262–267.
Kellam, S. G., Mackenzie, A. C., Brown, C. H., Poduska, J. M., Wang, W., Petras, H. et al. (2011). The good behavior game and the future of prevention and treatment. *Addiction Science and Clinical Practice, 6*(1), 73–84.
McGovern, M. P., Saunders, E. C., & Kim, E. (2013). Substance abuse treatment implementation research. *Journal of Substance Abuse Treatment, 44*(1), 1–3.
McKay, J. R. (2009). Continuing care research: What we have learned and where we are going. *Journal of Substance Abuse Treatment, 36*(2), 131–145.
McLellan, A. T., Carise, D., & Kleber, H. D. (2003). Can the national addiction treatment infrastructure support the public's demand for quality care? *Journal of Substance Abuse Treatment, 25*(2), 117–121.
McLellan, A. T., Lewis, D. C., O'Brien, C. P., and Kleber, H. D. (2000). Drug dependence, a chronic medical illness: Implications for treatment, insurance, and outcomes evaluation. *Journal of the American Medical Association, 263*, 13, 1689–1695.
McLellan, A. T., & Meyers, K. (2004). Contemporary addiction treatment: A review of systems problems for adults and adolescents. *Biological Psychiatry, 56*(10), 764–770.
Marr, C. and Brunet, G. (2009). Reversing the erosion in alcohol taxes could help pay for health care reform. Center on Budget and Policy Priorities. http://www.cbpp.org/cms/?fa=view&id=2828 (accessed 23 June 2013)
Martino, S., Brigham, G. S., Higgins, C., Gallon, S., Freese, T. E., Albright, L. M. et al. (2010). Partnerships and pathways of dissemination: The national institute on drug Abuse—Substance abuse and mental health services administration blending initiative in the clinical trials network. *Journal of Substance Abuse Treatment, 38*, S31–S43.
Meier, P. S., Barrowclough, C., & Donmall, M. C. (2005). The role of the therapeutic alliance in the treatment of substance misuse: A critical review of the literature. *Addiction, 100*(3), 304–316.
Miller, W. R. and Rollnick, S. (1991). *Motivational interviewing*. New York, NY: Guilford Press.
Miller, W. R. and Rollnick, S. (2002). *Motivational interviewing*, 2nd edition, New York, NY: Guilford Press.

Miller, W. R., Sorensen, J. L., Selzer, J. A., & Brigham, G. S. (2006). Disseminating evidence-based practices in substance abuse treatment: A review with suggestions. *Journal of Substance Abuse Treatment, 31*(1), 25–39.

Miller, W. R., Walter, S. T. and Bennett, M. E. (2001). How effective is alcoholism treatment in the United States? *Journal of Studies on Alcohol, 62*, 211–220.

Mitchell, O., Wilson, D. B., Eggers, A., & MacKenzie, D. L. (2012). Assessing the effectiveness of drug courts on recidivism: A meta-analytic review of traditional and non-traditional drug courts. *Journal of Criminal Justice, 40*(1), 60–71.

National Center on Addiction and Substance Abuse at Columbia University. (2010). Behind bars II: Substance abuse and America's prison population. New York, NY: National Center on Addiction and Substance Abuse at Columbia University.

National Institute on Alcohol Abuse and Alcoholism. (2006). *Alcohol use and alcohol use disorders in the United States: Main findings from the 2001–2002 survey on alcohol and related conditions (NESARC)*. Bethesda, MD: National Institute on Alcohol Abuse and Alcoholism.

Nielsen, A. L. and Scarpitti, F. R. (1997). Changing the behavior of substance abusers: Factors influencing the effectiveness of therapeutic communities. *Journal of Drug Issues, 27*, 279–298.

Nunes, E. V. (2011). The design and analysis of multisite effectiveness trials: A decade of progress in the national drug abuse clinical trials network. *American Journal of Drug and Alcohol Abuse, 37*(5), 269–272.

Office of National Drug Control Policy, Executive Office of the President. (2009). *ADAM II 2008 annual report. Arrestee Drug Abuse Monitoring Program II*. Washington, DC: Office of National Drug Control Policy, Executive Office of the President.

Pears, K., Capaldi, D. M., & Owen, L. D. (2007). Substance abuse risk across three generations: The roles of parent discipline practices and inhibitory control. *Psychology of Addictive Behaviors, 21*(3), 373–386.

Rieckmann, T., Farentinos, C., Tillotson, C., Kocarnik, J., & McCarty, D. (2011). The substance abuse counseling workforce: Education, preparation, and certification. *Substance Abuse, 32*(4), 180–190.

Robinson, M. B. and Scherlen, R. G. (2007). *Lies, damned lies, and drug war statistics: a critical analysis of claims made by the office of National Drug Control Policy*. Albany, NY: State University Press.

Roman, P. M., Abraham, A. J., Rothrauff, T. C., & Knudsen, H. K. (2010). A longitudinal study of organizational formation, innovation adoption, and dissemination activities within the national drug abuse treatment clinical trials network. *Journal of Substance Abuse Treatment, 38*, S44–S52.

Ryan, S. M., Jorm, A. F., & Lubman, D. I. (2010). Parenting factors associated with reduced adolescent alcohol use: A systematic review of longitudinal studies. *Australian and New Zealand Journal of Psychiatry, 44*(9), 774–783.

Salaspuro, M. (2003) Intervention against hazardous alcohol consumption – Secondary prevention of alcohol problems. In M. Berglund, S. Thelander, & E. Jonsson (Eds.), *Treating alcohol and drug abuse: An evidence-based review* (pp. 1–41). Weinheim: Wiley.

Santa Ana, E. J., Martino, S., Ball, S. A., Nich, C., Frankforter, T. L., & Carroll, K. M. (2008). What is usual about 'treatment-as-usual'? data from two multisite effectiveness trials. *Journal of Substance Abuse Treatment, 35*(4), 369–379.

Scott, C. K. & Dennis, M. L. (2011). Recovery management checkups with adult chronic substance users. In J. F. Kelly & W. L. White (Eds.), *Addiction recovery management: Theory, research, and practice* (pp. 87–101). Totowa, NJ: Humana Press.

Smith, D. E. (2012). Prescribing practices and the prescription drug epidemic: Physician intervention strategies. *Journal of Psychoactive Drugs, 44*(1), 68–71.

Smith, J. E., Meyers, R. J., & Miller, W. R. (2001). The community reinforcement approach to the treatment of substance use disorders. *American Journal on Addictions, 10*, 51–59.

Sobell, L. C. (2007). The phenomenon of self-change: Overview and key issues. In H. Klingermann and L. C. Sobell (Eds.), *Promoting self-change from addictive behavior: Practical implications for policy, prevention, and treatment* (pp. 1–30). New York: Springer.

Stockwell, P.. Gruenewald, J. W. Toumbourou, and W. Loxley (Eds.). (2005). *Preventing harmful substance use: The evidence base for policy and practice*. Chichester: Wiley.

Substance Abuse and Mental Health Services Administration. (2010). *Results from the 2009 National Survey on Drug Use and Health: Volume I. Summary of National Findings*. Rockville, MD: Office of Applied Studies.

Substance Abuse and Mental Health Services Administration. (2013). National Registry of evidence-based practices. http://www.nrepp.samhsa.gov/ (accessed 22 January 2012).

Substance Abuse and Mental Health Services Administration, Center for Behavioral Health Statistics and Quality. (2011). *Drug Abuse Warning Network, 2008: National estimates of drug-related emergency department visits*. Rockville, MD: HHS Publications.

Tai, B., Straus, M. M., Liu, D., Sparenborg, S., Jackson, R., & McCarty, D. (2010). The first decade of the national drug abuse treatment clinical trials network: Bridging the gap between research and practice to improve drug abuse treatment. *Journal of Substance Abuse Treatment*, *38*, S4–S13.

Toumbourou, J. W., Williams, J., & Patton, G. (2005). What do we know about preventing drug-related harm through social developmental intervention with children and young people? In T. Stockwell, P. J. Gruenewald, J.W. Toumbourou, & W. Loxley (Eds.), *Preventing harmful substance use: The evidence base for policy and practice* (pp. 87–100). Chichester: Wiley.

Welsh, W. N. (2007). A multisite evaluation of prison-based therapeutic community drug treatment. *Criminal Justice and Behavior*, *34*(11), 1481–1498.

Wexler, H. K., & Williams, R. (1986). The stay'n out therapeutic community: Prison treatment for substance abuse. *Journal of Psychoactive Drugs*, *18*, 221–230.

Whitlock, E. P., Polen, M. R., Green, C. A., Orleans, T., & Klein, J. (2004). Behavioral counseling interventions in primary care to reduce risky/harmful alcohol use by adults: A summary of the evidence for the U.S. preventive services task force. *Annals of Internal Medicine*, *140*(7), 557–580.

Yalisove, D. L. (1998). The origins and evolution of the disease concept of treatment. *Journal of Studies on Alcohol*, *59*, 469–476.

Ziegler, P. P., Goldenbaum, P., & Donald, M. (2011). Prescription drug abuse and diversion in clinical practice: What can be learned from from regulatory sanction data. *Journal of Addictions Nursing*, *22* (1–2), 13–18.

Zucker, R. A. (2008). Anticipating problem alcohol use developmentally from childhood into middle adulthood: What have we learned? *Addiction*, *103*, 100–108.

Alcohol, risks and public policy

Thom Brooks

Introduction

Alcohol occupies an important place in Western societies. It is difficult to imagine a return to prohibition as popular or even possible. Nevertheless, alcohol is often a presence in crime. Or stated differently, many crimes are committed by persons who have consumed alcohol and perhaps while under its influence. Alcohol might be considered a double-edged sword as something we use when celebrating positive achievements, such as a new job or marriage, but also something used where others engage in crime. Perhaps alcohol should still be permitted, but its use brings risks that may bear on public policy-makers.

This chapter examines the relation of risks and public policy through the lens of alcohol and crime. Alcohol leads a double-life as a fountain of celebration, but also a wellspring of potentially serious harms. Our question is how associated risks from its use might be managed much better. This question is approached through considering three different arenas each within the broad remit of English criminal law although addressing broader issues of criminal justice more widely. The first area is drunkenness and criminal liability. The second area considers the option of an additional tax on alcohol per unit. The last arena examined is a consideration of whether nudges might be more effect. The chapter concludes that the criminal law is a crude mechanism for grappling with complex issues of criminal responsibility for any higher risks associated with becoming under the influence. In short, the legal position is fairly intolerant and this has advantages in terms of administering justice. Higher taxation through so-called 'sin taxes' might also bring advantages, but there remain serious concerns to address as well. Perhaps an underexplored area for public policy decision-making is designing better 'nudges'. This is examined and defended below.

Drunkenness and criminal liability

Let us begin with the use of the criminal law to address problems of alcohol and the risk of criminal harms. While the criminal law is a crude mechanism for public policy-making, it largely and generally speaking gets the balance correct. This is not to claim there are no problems and these will be considered shortly.

Most non-lawyers mistakenly think the law is essentially retributivist. This is the view where criminals are punished to the degree deserved for the harms they expose or inflict to others (Moore, 1997). One problem with this view is that it assumes a strong connection between desert, understood as 'moral responsibility', and harm. This is captured in a crime, such as murder, where there is a requirement of specific intent connected to the cause of someone's death. But how to balance high moral responsibility for low risk of harm or low moral responsibility for high risk of harm? Retribution lacks clear answers to such cases where these elements move in contrary directions (Brooks, 2012).

But there is a more fundamental problem with the retributivist view of 'harm'. The kinds of harms that occupy the criminal law are not exclusively moral in nature (Brooks, 2013a). Not all crimes require proof of moral responsibility. One illustration is crimes of strict liability, perhaps the most numerous kind of criminal offence. Strict liability crimes include traffic offences (including illegal parking and speeding) and drug offences (such as heroin possession) where the offence is proved where there is evidence someone, in fact, drove a car beyond a clearly demarcated speed limit or was found to possess heroin. Broader circumstances pertaining to moral decision-making are irrelevant for confirming these offences.

Nonetheless, retribution exercises a powerful grip on the popular imagination and not without good reason. There are less numerous, but more serious crimes in which moral responsibility can play an important role in helping us determining whether that crime was committed. Plus, the moral responsibility of offenders also pertains to our assessment of harmful risks. So, for example, arson is a crime with a potentially significant prison sentence for arsonists because arson is no mere mistake, but a purposeful activity and it includes a view to its potentially deadly risk or exposure to serious harm. The common view that criminals should be punished to the degree they deserve for the risk of harms they present to others may be factually untrue, but there is some basis in fact among the crimes that grab popular headlines most from murder to arson and beyond.

There are several established links between alcohol consumption and crime (Popovici et al., 2012). For example, both violent and non-violent crimes are linked with the density of local businesses offering alcoholic products for sale (Toomey et. al., 2012a, 2012b), including domestic violence (Livingstone, 2011). The evidence is that the higher the density of such businesses, we can expect to find higher numbers of these offences. There is also a more specific link identified between binge drinking and sexual assault where the presence of the former is connected with a greater risk of the latter (Abbey, 2002; Franklin 2011; Mouilso, Fischer, & Calhoun, 2012; Rothman et al., 2012). We examine approaches to addressing this link between alcohol consumption and criminal risks beyond the criminal law in the sections below. Our focus here is on the criminal law.

In England and Wales, criminal offences have three different standards of relevant intent. The first we have already considered are crimes of strict liability where no intent by the accused need be proved to confirm her conviction for that crime. So the bare fact that a car was driven by that person above the clearly demarcated speed limit is necessary and sufficient to secure conviction for this crime. Strict liability crimes are the majority of offences found in the criminal law.

Other offences are divided roughly into crimes of specific or basic intent. Crimes requiring proof of fault, or *mens rea*, are at least crimes of basic intent. So a person can be convicted of wounding or inflicting grievous bodily harm (section 20 of the Offences Against the Person Act (OAPA) 1861) through the bare fact that this person was responsible for causing such harm to another. This is an example of a crime of basic intent. A crime of specific intent is where a more narrow and particular intention is required to prove the offence. An illustration is wounding, or causing grievous bodily harm with intent to do grievous bodily harm (section 18 of OAPA 1861). This crime is different in kind because it rests not on the bare fact that the accused *caused* harm, but that he *intended* to cause the harm that transpired. This difference is captured by the fact that crimes of basic intent often have lower maximum tariffs than crimes of specific intent. So causing grievous bodily harm to another (without specific intent) does have a less punitive maximum sentence than causing grievous bodily harm with an intent to do so. These different offence types possess different possible outcomes. It could be argued that one reason for this difference is the fact of a specific intent to do harm to others makes the activity of greater potential harmful risk in keeping with a broadly retributivist perspective.

The consumption of alcohol is relevant here because it can affect convictions for offences. Intoxication can negate specific intent, but not always. That someone is drunk and engages in harmful conduct under the influence of drugs or alcohol can mean this person receives a conviction for inflicting grievous bodily harm, but not intending to do so. However, if this person possessed the intent to cause harm to another prior to intoxication, his being intoxication would not negate the specific intent he has: intoxication can be a barrier to creating *new* specific intents, but it need not *erase* existing specific intents already possessed.[1]

The wider point is that *voluntary* intoxication is no defence when faced with conviction for a crime. However, this can be a mitigating factor when determining sentencing and other criminal justice outcomes. Being under the influence is no legal excuse for engaging in criminal activity in general. This may run counter to popular perceptions about retribution and moral responsibility. It might be asked: how can someone be fully responsible for their actions when under the influence of drugs and alcohol?

The law's answer is that we hold others to account for the exposure or imposition of harmful risks with only narrow exceptions. It is *because* intoxication is so often present in criminal cases that it can play little, if any, factor in confirming convictions and generally only relevant for sentencing.

The law does make an exception for *involuntary* intoxication, but such cases can be rare and there are a number of conditions. For example, someone *is* involuntarily intoxicated if he is intoxicated unknowingly, but not if he is knowingly consuming an intoxicating substance. So a person is involuntarily intoxicated if they think they are drinking pure orange juice when it is, in fact, spiked with vodka. But this person is *not* involuntarily intoxicated if they think they are drinking beer when it is, in fact, spiked with vodka or whisky. When a person is, in law, involuntarily intoxicated, this can provide evidence to help establish a full defence, such as automatism (Law Commission, 2009). Note that a person is not involuntarily intoxicated in law every time he or she is intoxicated unknowingly, such as where a known alcoholic product has been spiked to make it more potent.

Alcohol is demonstrated to have links with risks, such as higher risks of criminal offences. The criminal law allows only a narrow exception for cases of involuntary intoxication. Otherwise, drunkenness is no excuse and persons under or not under the influence can both be held criminally liable for al strict liability and basic intent offences.

Reducing risks through higher taxation

A second option for reducing risks is so-called 'sin taxes'. Or, more specifically, an additional or higher tax on alcoholic products. The argument is that higher prices will lead to less demand as scarce resources are spent on goods other than alcoholic products. There is evidence that such efforts can improve public health. One study found raising the price of alcoholic products by 6% led to reduced injury deaths by 4.5% (Cook & Durrance, 2013). Another study found 1% increase in the cost of alcoholic products led to an increase of nearly 6.5 days where no alcohol is consumed (Byrnes et al., 2013). The evidence is clear: higher prices will lead to less consumption and less consumption will lead to fewer alcohol-related problems. So is higher taxation the answer? The answer may not be so conclusive.

The taxation of alcohol is usually defended as a tax on per unit of alcohol in a product. The effect is to increase the cost of alcoholic products with a greater impact on products with higher units of alcohol. So a bottle of wine (about nine units) would face a much higher cost increase than a pint of weak ale (two2 units) (NHS, 2013). Adding a tax of £1 per unit would increase the average cost of a bottle of wine from about £5 to £14 and increase the average cost of a pint of ale from about £3 to £5.

An increase in the price of alcoholic products per unit could be an effective policy solution if the use of certain alcoholic products were strongly linked with criminality. But there is no such established link between the higher the units of alcohol in a particular alcoholic product and risk of criminal activity. In the absence of more specific information, increasing the price of units can be a crude device for driving down alcohol consumption overall. But a more effective policy aiming to reduce risks and criminal activity might more clearly target those products most associated with the problem to be tackled. And it is likely true that those products most affected, such as a bottle of single-malt whisky, might be less associated with criminal behaviour linked with alcohol use than products with fewer units.

If we accept that the more units of alcohol a person has consumed the more likely he is to engage in criminal activity, then what should be our policy? It would appear that ensuring individuals consumed fewer units would contribute to less criminal activity. But that is only at the *macro* level looking across individual activity as a whole without looking more carefully at their particular behaviours. What we require is a more specific link between *types* of product and *crime*. The point is that it may be more effective to target the potential risks from using specific products to better pinpoint improvements to addressing criminal activity. The issue is not only that alcohol is consumed as different alcoholic products may expose individuals to different risks than others independently of their alcoholic strength. There is a need to better identify links at the *micro* level between product types and criminal offence types. So perhaps less alcohol consumption at a macro level can lead to improvements in public health for many individuals, but this remains a crude mechanism for addressing the different risks from different products. Or stated differently: perhaps improvements in public health and criminal justice policy at a *macro* level can be achieved by a blanket imposition of higher taxes per unit because this help cause consumption of fewer units across the general population. This mistakes the problem as higher unit consumption *in general* where the problem might be the consumption of *specific product types* in particular.

This reveals a second type of taxation. Recall the first type is to increase the costs of alcoholic products in relation to their alcoholic strengths by a tax per unit. This one-size-fits-all approach fails to address the very different effects and potential risks that different products might have independently of their alcoholic strength. The second type is to increase costs, to reduce availability, of specific types of product.

Suppose one product (*a*) has twice the alcoholic strength in a serving than a second product (*b*). Should *a* be taxed higher than *b*? One reply is yes so that macro levels of alcoholic consumption are reduced. And perhaps this is the easiest, if more crude, way of delivering an important public good. But a second reply is no and perhaps the situation should be reversed. This is because consumers of *b* are far more likely to engage in riskier behaviour and criminal activity. So the reduction of alcohol-related risks and crime might be more effective on targeting those alcoholic products more associated with crime. Perhaps there would be fewer offenders if fewer units were consumed, but it matters which units *of what* are consumed if we are to more effectively contribute to targeting this problem.

This is not to deny more philosophical issues about the moral justification and desirability of minimum pricing through higher taxes on units of alcohol or particular kinds of alcoholic product (Saunders, 2013). For example, one significant disadvantage of taxation approaches in this area is their *effects* assume a *standardised person*. Or, in other words, this policy assumes we, the citizens affected, occupy a substantively similar position in relation to each other. In truth, there may be significant inequality whereby higher prices for consumable goods we all enjoy will become no less difficult for some to consume and effectively banned for those with less expenditure money. Reducing consumption of certain (or all) products might disproportionately affect the lifestyles and/or pursuit of preferred leisure activities by some demographics than others. Crime is not only linked with alcohol use and so perhaps additional justification is warranted for policies that might contribute to a wider public good for all (e.g., less crime) by increasing burdens on some and not all.

Nudges – the future?

Richard Thaler and Cass Sunstein (2008) have popularised the idea of so-called 'nudges' exposing the public policy implications of behavioural economics.[2] Thaler and Sunstein consider a range of policy proposals for improving public health, individual wealth and personal happiness that have attracted much interest and not inconsiderable controversy (Saint-Paul, 2011). Nevertheless, one area that is relatively underexplored is the ways through which risky, and potentially criminal, behaviour could be better managed through the use of nudges.

One illustration by Thaler and Sunstein of a nudge to reduce alcohol consumption is what they call 'socializing nondrinking' (2008: 73). They focus on the case study of binge drinking by university students. Surveys consistently report a significant problem of such behaviour and its effects across campuses. One nudge is to communicate that such behaviour is non-standard and exceptional. So an illustration would be to advertise that the average student drinks only a few units of alcohol per week, for example. The idea is that new students can become socialised into risky, binge-drinking behaviour where they perceive such activities are normal and common. We can provide a nudge by correcting this information and helping them realise that what is normal and common is very different from the perceptions new students may have acquired from fiction or movies about campus life. If students knew more about how other students really are, then binge drinking would be seen as more exceptional and might occur much less often. We can tackle binge drinking effectively by helping students gain more accurate information to permit more informed decision-making. By improving information about choices, we can improve the choices made and so reduce binge drinking without other interventionist policies.

But there are other nudges we can employ to help reduce alcohol consumption and we will briefly survey them now. One option is to support new regulations concerning advertising in line with the policy to tackle binge drinking on university campuses. There have been great strides in helping communicate the problems of drink driving in recent years and similar efforts can and should be fed into informing the public that drinking is a right that comes with responsibilities.

A second option is to reconsider where alcoholic products can be placed in shops. Thaler and Sunstein (2008: 1–2) note that children can make more healthy choices about what to eat by rearranging their options at a cafeteria. Healthier foods should be placed at the front, at eye level and easy to reach while less healthy foods should be placed towards the end of the queue and made less accessible. Similarly, alcoholic products can be placed not at eye-level and made more difficult to access, such as behind the cashier. This does not deny anyone access to alcoholic products if they are legally entitled to consume them, but it can be a nudge against making such a choice.

A third option concerns individual sales transactions involving alcoholic products. Many of us today purchase products using debit or credit cards. Cashiers have machines into which we insert our cards and then sign or enter a pin code to make a transaction. These can be reconfigured so that purchases of alcoholic products might trigger a new screen requiring confirmation before the purchase is approved, such as asking customers if they are aware they are purchasing an alcoholic product or perhaps a general warning about the recommended maximum number of units to be consumed in a week. A fourth option is improved labelling that more clearly identify potential public health issues and risks.

The costs of these regulations to consumers and companies trading in alcoholic products would be negligible, but the benefits to public health and wider policy could be considerable – and without a focus on reducing consumption, but rather improving how alcoholic products are consumed. We can provide effective nudges that can reduce consumption without reducing consumer choice.

Conclusion

This chapter examines alcohol and public policy through the dimension of risks and criminal justice. While alcohol occupies a central place in 'our' celebrations in the West, alcohol has similar dominating place in the harms endured by too many through criminal activities. The issue concerns drawing lines about how a more satisfactory balance of risks might be struck.

This issue has been approached here through several angles. The first is the criminal law. We have seen that the criminal law is a crude instrument making few exceptions. A second angle considered is taxation. We have seen this is often operationalised through a higher tax per unit to help cut consumption and contribute to benefit improvements to public health and reducing crime. But this is a fairly crude measure as well often aimed at *macro*-level activity where a more effective policy should target alcohol consumption at the *micro*-level, such as targeting particular kinds of product most associated with problematic behaviours.

The final consideration is the use of so-called nudges. However else elusive, there are under-explored ways through which risky, and potentially criminal, behaviour could be better managed through the use of nudges. If we wish to reduce overuse without limiting supply, then several options are raised such as new regulations concerning advertising, the place of alcoholic products in shops, individual sales transactions involving alcoholic products and improved labelling. The costs of these regulations to consumers and companies trading in alcoholic products would be negligible, but the benefits to public health and wider policy could be considerable – and without a focus on reducing consumption, but rather improving how alcoholic products are consumed.

In conclusion, the argument is not that we should endorse a nudge-only approach to alcohol and public policy, but that nudges could and should play a much greater role than they do in improving public policy in this area in concert with existing policy concerning criminal law and taxation. Together, the risks of alcohol consumption can be better managed if only we more willing – and *more imaginative* – about how we might provide nudges and reduce risks.

Notes

1. Kingston [1995] 2 AC 355, [1994] 3 WLR 519.
2. See Brooks (2013b).

References

Abbey, A. (2002). Alcohol-related sexual assault: A common problem among college students. *Journal of Studies on Alcohol*, *14*, 118–128.

Brooks, T. (2012). *Punishment*. London: Routledge.

Brooks, T. (2013a). Criminal harms. In *Law and Legal Theory*. Boston, MA: Leiden.

Brooks, T. (2013b). Should we nudge informed consent? *American Journal of Bioethics*, *13*, 22–23.

Byrnes, J., Shakeshaft, A., Petrie, D., & Doran, C. (2013). Can harms associated with high-intensity drinking be reduced by increasing the price of alcohol? *Drug and Alcohol Review*, *32*, 27–30.

Cook, P. J., & Durrance, C. P. (2013). The virtuous tax: Lifesaving and crime-prevention effects of the 1991 Federal alcohol-tax increase. *Journal of Health Economics*, *32*, 261–67.

Franklin, C. A. (2011). An investigation of the relationship between self-control and alcohol induced sexual assault victimization. *Criminal Justice and Behavior*, *38*, 263–285.

Law Commission. (2009). *Intoxication and Criminal Responsibility*. London: Stationery Office.

Livingstone, M. (2011). A longitudinal analysis of alcohol outlet density and domestic violence. *Addiction*, *106*, 919–925.

Moore, M. (1997). *Placing blame*. Oxford: Clarendon.
Mouilso, E. R., Fischer, S., & Calhoun, K. S. (2012). A prospective study of sexual assault and alcohol use among first-year college women. *Violence and Victims*, *27*, 78–94.
National Health Service (NHS). (2013). Alcohol units. http://www.nhs.uk/Livewell/alcohol/Pages/alcohol-units.aspx.
Popovici, I., Homer, J. F., Fang, H., & French, M. T. (2012). Alcohol use and crime: Findings from a longitudinal sample of U.S. adolescents and young adults. *Alcoholism – Clinical and Experimental Research*, *36*, 532–543.
Rothman, E. F., Reyes, L. M., Johnson, R. M., & LaValley, M. (2012). Does the alcohol make them do it? Dating violence perpetration and drinking among youth. *Epidemiologic Reviews*, *34*, 103–119.
Saint-Paul, G. (2011). *The tyranny of utility: Behavioral social science and the rise of paternalism*. Princeton, NJ: Princeton University Press.
Saunders, B. (2013). Minimum pricing for alcohol: a Millian perspective. *Contemporary Social Science*, *8*, 71–82.
Thaler, R. H., & Sunstein, C. R. (2008). *Nudge: Improving decisions about health, wealth and happiness*. Harmondsworth: Penguin.
Toomey, T. L., Erickson, D. J., Carlin, B. P., Lenk, K. M., Quick, H. S., Jones, A. M. et al. (2012a). The association between density of alcohol establishments and violent crime within urban neighborhoods. *Alcoholism – Clinical and Experimental Research*, *36*, 1468–1473.
Toomey, T. L., Erickson, D. J., Carlin, B. P., Quick, H. S., Harwood, E. M., Lenk, K. M. et al. (2012b). Is the density of alcohol establishments related to nonviolent crime? *Journal of Studies on Alcohol and Drugs*, *73*, 21–25.

Socially Responsible Investment in the alcohol industry: an assessment of investor attitudes and ethical arguments

Boudewijn de Bruin

Faculties of Economics and Business and Philosophy, University of Groningen, Groningen, The Netherlands

I examine and evaluate the ethical standards and arguments that Socially Responsible Investment (SRI) investors use when they deselect the alcohol industry and alcohol corporations. The alcohol industry was the first industry excluded by SRI investors and is, relative to fund size, the second most prominent negative screen (after tobacco). I discuss the role of shareholder democracy in the alcohol industry, review some evidence on the financial effects of SRI on sin stocks and investigate the motivations that SRI investors may have to eschew investment in the alcohol industry (almost no motivation can be found). I discuss a number of ethical issues that are salient in the alcohol industry and that ought to concern ethical investors. I draw attention to, in particular, the marketing of alcopops (flavoured alcoholic beverages or malternatives such as Smirnoff Ice and Bacardi Breezer), and strategies involving so-called beer girls. This prepares the way to a reconstruction of two kinds of arguments that SRI investors might implicitly adhere to when they put a negative screen on alcohol: a Public Goods Argument and a Religious Values Argument. I show that the Public Goods Argument is problematic because it risks democratic legitimacy and effectiveness, and that while the Religious Values Argument is a coherent defence for individual investors accepting particular religious views, it is unacceptable if used by institutional investors forcing religious values upon involuntary participants when no societal unanimity concerning these religious values exists. Pension funds and health-care plans are examples of such investors. Finally, I provide an alternative Ethical Issues Argument and defend the claim that there are no good moral reasons for institutional SRI investors to circumvent the alcohol industry; rather, they should use shareholder democracy to make alcohol corporations address the ethical issues lest these issues will never be addressed by the corporations themselves.

Introduction

Socially Responsible Investment (SRI) is a booming business. But is it an ethical business? And if so, what sort of ethics is it that inspires SRI? A poll among SRI research analysts delivered the following top list: Dell, Gap, General Mills, Hewlett-Packard, Intel, Southwest Airlines, Starbucks and Timberland (Kurtz, 2009). We could offer the following glosses: Dell (fined $100 million for an accounting scandal), Gap (accused of sourcing from child sweatshops), General Mills (seems scandal-free recently), Hewlett-Packard (CEO retreated on charges of sexual harassment), Intel (fined a record $1.44 billion for monopoly abuse), Southwest Airlines (serious issue about safety of more than one hundred planes), Starbucks (water waste scandal) and Timberland (seems scandal-free recently).

What ethical standards and arguments, if any, do SRI investors use when they select or deselect particular companies? And are these arguments adequate? In this article, I answer this question with respect to one particular industry – alcohol corporations. The alcohol industry was the first industry excluded by SRI investors (by Methodists in the eighteenth century) (Kurtz, 2009). With tobacco and gambling, alcohol forms the *Triumvirate of Sin* (Hong & Kacperczyk, 2009). Relative to fund size, alcohol is the second most prominent *negative screen* (after tobacco) employed by SRI investors, which means a great number of them completely exclude the alcohol industry, irrespective of the particular company, kind of beverage, sort of marketing or the company's environmental, social or governance record and irrespective of whether the company is involved in alcohol manufacturing, licensing, retailing or in the manufacturing of products that are a prerequisite for the production of alcoholic beverages or whether the company owns an alcohol company or whether it is being owned (as a company) by an alcohol company.

Alcohol-related mortality amounts to 2.3 million people a year worldwide (Worth Health Organization, 2011), and no one can sensibly deny that alcohol poses a massive health problem to a significant number of people. I argue, however, that there is no justification of the sort of negative screens used by many SRI investors, except the religious one embraced by, among others, Islamic investors. In the first three sections of the paper, I discuss the role of shareholder democracy in the alcohol industry, I review some evidence on the financial effects of SRI on *sin stocks*, and I investigate the motivations that SRI investors may have to eschew investment in the alcohol industry (almost no motivation can be found). Subsequently, I discuss a number of ethical issues that are salient in the alcohol industry and that ought to concern ethical investors. I draw attention to, in particular, the marketing of *alcopops* (flavoured alcoholic beverages or *malternatives* such as Smirnoff Ice and Bacardi Breezer) and strategies involving so-called *beer girls*. This prepares the way to a reconstruction of two kinds of arguments that SRI investors might implicitly adhere to when they put a negative screen on alcohol: a *Public Goods Argument* and a *Religious Values Argument*. I show that the Public Goods Argument is problematic because it risks democratic legitimacy and effectiveness, and that while the Religious Values Argument is a coherent defence for individual investors accepting particular religious views, it is unacceptable if used by institutional investors forcing religious values upon involuntary participants when no societal unanimity concerning these religious values exists. Pension funds and health-care plans are examples of such investors. Finally, I provide an alternative, the *Ethical Issues Argument*, which ultimately leads me to defend the claim that there are no good moral reasons for institutional SRI investors to circumvent the alcohol industry; rather, they should use shareholder democracy to make alcohol corporations address the ethical issues lest these issues will never be addressed by the corporations themselves.

Shareholder democracy

The phenomenon that shareholders influence corporate policy and that they are part of the corporate decision-making process has been described as a form of *shareholder democracy* (Parkinson, 1993). How far shareholder democracy extends depends to a large extent on the rights and duties that come with being a shareholder. Even though shareholders are seen as the owners of the corporation, corporate ownership is different from most other forms of ownership in several important respects. Unlike ownership of a house or a car, ownership of a firm is extremely fragmented because most firms are owned by a great many different shareholders. Because shares are generally easily transferable, corporate ownership changes continuously, and unlike houses or cars, firms are controlled by boards of directors to which the shareholders have delegated management. The owners themselves are only distantly involved in decision-making. As a result, the rights of shareholders are a far cry from the rights of owners of houses and cars.

A truncated form of ownership does not rule out shareholder democracy, though. Shareholders not only possess the right to sell their shares and the right to certain residual earnings when the company bankrupts, but also have the right to vote in the general meeting, the right to obtain information from the company and the right to file lawsuits against management (Monks & Minow, 2004). Moreover, because of the very specific way in which shareholders delegate decision-making, directors have a number of duties vis-à-vis the shareholders, including the duty to act for the benefit of the company and the duties of care and diligence (Parkinson, 1993). Shareholder rights and management duties, it is hoped, will help solving the agency problems inherent in the relation between shareholders and management.

But sometimes shareholder rights have to be exercised with vigour. One form shareholder democracy may assume is called *shareholder activism*. Activist shareholders are shareholders actively try to influence corporate decision-making by discussing issues with management, by getting shareholder resolutions accepted and by filing lawsuits against management. As Sparkes (2001) notes, activist shareholders come in many shapes. Like Gordon Gekko in his notorious 'Greed is Good' speech in Oliver Stone's *Wall Street* film, some activists are motivated by financial interests only and attempt to change management of what they consider to be companies that under-perform. Others, however, buy shares of a company with the sole reason to be able to voice concerns about environmental or social issues at the general meeting and to attract attention from the media. This form of shareholder activism is called *advocacy campaigning* (Sparkes, 2001), *engagement* (O'Rourke, 2003) or *dialogue* (Mackenzie, 1998).

A quick scan of the coverage by the *Financial Times* and the *Wall Street Journal* of the 10 largest beer companies and the 10 largest spirits companies over the last 10 years reveals that advocacy campaigning in the alcohol industry is rare. Shareholder activism in the alcohol industry addresses the common themes of executive remuneration, corporate strategy, mergers and acquisitions or ineffective competition, but genuine advocacy campaigning addressing environmental and social issues is almost entirely absent. A widely publicised case involves Thai Beverage, a Thai brewery and whisky producer, one of the 10 largest worldwide, facing heavy street protests from Buddhist monks in front of the Thai stock exchange when it announced it would enter the Thai stock market (Leoywanichjalearn, 2012). But since the monks were no shareholders of the company, this is strictly speaking not a form of advocacy campaigning. More detailed and rigorous research would have to test these initial findings, but given the fact that part of what motivates advocacy campaigning is to receive media attention, the lack of international financial media coverage does suggest, I believe, that advocacy campaigning in the alcohol industry is not very frequent.

If it is specifically ethical investors who engage in advocacy campaigning, then the low incidence of advocacy campaigning in the alcohol industry may be explained by the fact that a significant portion of ethical investors abstain from buying alcohol shares altogether. And if you do not have shares, you cannot engage in advocacy campaigning. These ethical investors exercise another and more radical form of shareholder democracy, namely, SRI. Cowton (1994) defines SRI as 'the exercise of ethical and social criteria in the selection and management of investment portfolios, generally consisting of company shares' (p. 215), and later included 'more conventional financial criteria' in the definition as well (Cowton, 1999, p. 60).

SRI investors use several techniques to select assets. *Negative screening* and *positive screening* refers to the practice of avoiding or including firms on the basis of their matching particular negative or positive criteria. Almost all large US social investors, for instance, have a negative screen on tobacco, and many screen against alcohol (Social Investment Forum Foundation, 2010). In the finance literature, screens involving the Triumvirate of Sin (alcohol, gambling, tobacco) are frequently studied, but other negative screens can be found excluding the sex industry, defence, abortion and birth control, animal rights, child labour, environmental hazards, nuclear power, employee rights, among others (Crane & Matten, 2010). Positive screens, in turn, aim at selecting firms that are progressive with respect to such environmental, social and governance criteria, and include things such as green technology, diversity and so on.

An alternative technique used by SRI investors is that of *relative selection* (Louche & Lydenberg, 2010). Rather than excluding firms or entire sectors upfront, a best-in-class approach is used, selecting those firms within a sector that score best on environmental, social and governance criteria. The well-known Dow Jones Sustainability Index uses a best-in-class approach based on work by SAM Sustainability Investing (2012). Sin stocks are, then, not excluded, witness the SAM Sector Leaders and Movers of 2012: Molson Coors Brewing (alcohol), TABCorp Holdings (gambling) and British American Tobacco (tobacco).

Finance

As Cowton's (1999) above-mentioned definition of SRI made clear, SRI criteria involve financial concerns as well. Practitioners sometimes claim that SRI funds perform better than regular funds in the long run. Kurtz (2009), however, casts doubt on this claim, observing that for an SRI fund to do better than regular funds, it would have to satisfy two conditions. First, it would have to be the case that higher levels of corporate social responsibility of the companies selected by the fund add significant economic value to the companies over time; and second, the financial markets would largely have to fail to perceive this added value. Kurtz (2009) claims that even if the first condition holds – and there is evidence that it does – it is unlikely that the second condition also holds because financial markets already expect above-average growth from companies selected by SRI funds with the result that the added economic value is already reflected in the price of the shares. SRI funds are just as good financially speaking as regular funds.

But what about the mirror image of SRI funds – vice funds and sin stocks? This question is particularly important for our present purposes because almost all definitions of vice funds and sin stocks include alcohol. Only a very scant literature deals with this question, though. In an influential article, Hong and Kacperczyk (2009) provide evidence to the effect that for the years 1965–2006 sin stocks have higher expected returns than comparable regular shares; they outperform their comparables by 29 basis points per month. Plainly put, and combining with Kurtz's (2009) findings, one may not lose by investing in SRI funds, but one may decidedly gain by singling out shares that are the opposite of SRI.

Perhaps even more importantly, Hong and Kacperczyk (2009) are the first to find decisive evidence for the claim that a particular group of investors do indeed avoid sin stocks. They find that pension funds, university endowments, foundations, religious organisations, banks and insurance companies and other investors that have relatively high public exposure and are potentially scrutinised by a large public invest less in sin stocks than investors such as mutual and hedge funds that operate more on the sidelines. While the two authors are cautious enough not to attribute this to the influence of SRI explicitly, they do take these figures to show that investors with high public visibility are more constrained by norms than others.

A serious question is whether all this applies to alcohol as well. The finance literature on sin stocks is still very slim, and to my knowledge no academic article has so far dealt with the alcohol industry in isolation. Nevertheless, some initial findings are coming forward. El Ghoul, Guedhami, Kwok, and Mishra (2011) studied a broader range of sin stocks than Hong and Kacperczyk (2009), but for the much shorter interval 1992–2007, and provided some evidence that unlike tobacco and nuclear power, alcohol, firearms and the military may not be significantly related to cost of capital. If that is true, the price of alcohol stocks would not reflect the fact that they are avoided by norm-constrained investors. El Ghoul et al. (2011) also found that not all SRI criteria are equally related to cost of capital. Taking a standard social performance index, they found that corporate social responsibility policies targeted at employee relations, environment and product strategies lower cost of capital, while community relations, diversity and human rights have no influence on the firm's cost of capital.

Neither of these studies should be considered conclusive. Salaber (2009), for instance, presents a number of very interesting results that somewhat go against the studies by Hong and Kacperczyk (2009) and El Ghoul et al. (2011), suggesting as she does that once a European database is adopted, rather different conclusions suggest themselves. She finds evidence, for instance, for a striking religious determinant, showing that while investors in Catholic countries seem not to avoid sin stocks, investors in Protestant countries do display *sin aversion*. This observation will be particularly relevant to the Religious Values Argument discussed later.

SRI investors

Hong and Kacperczyk (2009) give considerable attention to explaining the alleged sinfulness of investing in gambling and tobacco, but remain strikingly terse when it comes to alcohol. They merely observe that the sinfulness of alcohol 'has long been recognized by societies into which [it has] been introduced'. The brevity of their argument mirrors the lack of explicit argumentation on the part of SRI investors themselves.

How do SRI investors determine their selection criteria? Mackenzie (1998) distinguishes two ways in which SRI funds choose their criteria. *Market-led funds* adopt criteria provided by research institutions such as Ethical Investment Research Service (EIRIS) and SAM Sustainability Investing in the expectation that this allows them to set up funds that cater to the wishes of the consumer most effectively. They do not, that is, select assets on the basis of their own principles about environmental, social or governance issues, but are rather led by what the market considers as SRI. *Deliberative funds*, by contrast, engage in ethical deliberation themselves, either by means of in-house experts or by advisory committees.

Mackenzie (1998) provides an interesting argument against market-led funds. At first, he notes, market-led funds may argue that they leave the ethical deliberation to the individual investors themselves. The investor would develop a set of principles to guide their investment decisions and then select one or more corresponding SRI funds. On the basis of telephone interviews with ethical investors, Mackenzie claims that individual investors do not, however, take the pains to develop such ethical principles, but rather uncritically follow the criteria offered by the SRI funds on the market. As a result, market-led funds run the risk of being 'investments reflecting fashionable causes' (Anderson et al., 1996, cited by Mackenzie, 1998, p. 84).

But deliberative funds have their problems too. Mackenzie (1998) reports on the way in which Friends Provident Stewardship, the largest SRI fund in the UK at the time, would decide on its ethical criteria. A Committee of Reference consisting of six individuals with experience in business and corporate ethics would meet around four times a year for some five hours and would base their decisions on factual reports from EIRIS amounting to some 100 pages. This may seem impressive – but less so if one realises that a sustainability report of only one single company easily spans already more than 100 pages alone.

If selection criteria are not always too thoroughly argued, a second issue is whether SRI funds make the arguments they have for these criteria sufficiently transparent to the outside world. For religious funds, the defence is often rather straightforward, and many SRI funds have religious origins. The first SRI fund in the US was a Methodist fund, the Pax Fund, and going back almost 300 years, Kurtz (2009) describes John Wesley's sermons – the founding father of Methodism – as the 'first blueprint of socially responsible investment'. In his sermon on 'The Use of Money' (dated 1744 or 1760), Wesley starts with the observation that there is nothing inherently wrong with gaining money, but only potentially with the way it is used. He rather describes money as 'an excellent gift of God', and states as the first of four principles regulating the use money: 'Gain all you can!' The next three principles, then, qualify this maxim, stating that our gaining money should not endanger our own life, health and mind, nor the life, health and mind of our neighbour. Wesley makes abundantly clear that the principle not to harm one's neighbour's health forbids us to gain money from activities connected to the production and sales of alcoholic beverages, because distilleries 'murder His Majesty's subjects' and 'drive them to hell, like sheep'.

Considering the size of the funds, Wesley's remarks have caught on beyond Methodism. In the USA, only tobacco is a more important screen (Social Investment Forum Foundation, 2010).[1] The Dow Jones Sustainability Index and the FTSE4Good index both include the alcohol industry, though, and as we saw, Salaber's (2009) study uncovered important religious differences between the attitudes towards the alcohol industry. But we can only guess the motivations underlying these differences. As Mackenzie (1998) indicates, there is a striking lack of transparency on the part of the SRI funds about the reasons they adopt particular selection criteria. While most SRI funds clearly indicate their screening and relative selection criteria, they rarely offer consumers any insights in the motivation that underlies the adoption of the criteria. And while Mackenzie's (1998) study is now almost 15 years old, his conclusion still seems to be largely valid. Often used principles, such as the Equator Principles, the UN Principles of Responsible Investment or the information sites of organisations such as EIRIS, Eurosif, National Ethical Investment Week, Socialfunds.com or individual SRI funds, only rarely provide a clear argument why they do not invest in the alcohol industry.

Ethical issues

A useful way to categorise arguments that may be brought forward by individual and institutional investors against the alcohol industry distinguishes between the production of alcohol, the marketing of alcoholic beverages and the consumption of alcoholic drinks.

Environmental concerns about the production of alcoholic beverages include things such as the emission of carbon dioxide during fermentation processes, the management of waste (primarily the residue of fermentation), water and energy efficiency, packaging (bottles, cans) and shipping. For each bottle of beer, for instance, more than five bottles of water are used during production (Heineken, 2012). Some of these concerns relate to human rights and other issues, witness, for instance, a complaint by the Under-Secretary-General of the United Nations that Kenya Breweries consumes around 6% of the total water supply in Nairobi.[2] But these concerns seem not to be specific to the industry, and that is also true of other ethical issues including sexual harassment, occupational safety, the right to fair wages, misuse of power over suppliers, corruption, overly aggressive competition or collusion and so on.

This is not to say that there are no industry-specific ethical issues. To begin with, conflicts of interest may arise from collaboration of research institutes, non-governmental organisations or governmental agencies with the alcohol industry (Babor, Edwards, & Stockwell, 1996). A widely publicised case is the Global Fund to Fight AIDS, Tuberculosis and Malaria receiving a grant from SABMiller, one of the largest beer breweries, to carry out research on education programmes targeted at minimising harm related to alcohol consumption (Matzopoulos et al., 2012). And these concerns are not all unfounded if Bekelman, Li, and Gross (2003) is right that research sponsored by industry is almost four times as likely to provide positive results about a product.

Most ethical issues have to do with alcohol consumption, though. The costs of alcohol consumption are widely researched, and there is no need to give a detailed overview. Alcohol leads to 2.3 million deaths worldwide a year, is often involved in traffic accidents, crime and child protection cases, may lead to brain damage, decreased IQ, mental problems, addiction and aggression, liver cirrhosis, cancers, weakening of the immune system and alcohol is also implicated in HIV and tuberculosis contagion, among others (World Health Organization 2011). While these costs are significant and very serious, it is important to note that the literature tends to overlook the benefits derived from alcohol consumption. Most people derive pleasure from the consumption of alcohol. Moderate alcohol consumption is claimed to have particular health benefits including decreasing the likelihood of hypertension, reducing stress and certain geropsychiatric problems (Peele, 2000). Alcohol consumption fosters socialisation. Production, marketing and sales of alcoholic beverages provide employment. The UK industry, for instance, provides jobs to over 650,000 individuals in production and retail, and a further one million in the remainder of the economy (Wine and Spirit Trade Association, 2012). In the literature, these benefits are typically considered to be *private* (Godfrey, 2004), and hardly ever do researchers attempt to provide a monetary estimate of these benefits.

From the perspective of shareholder democracy, however, the marketing of alcoholic beverages is probably the most important issue, because it is in marketing that the industry has the largest power to mitigate the disadvantages of excessive or irresponsible alcohol consumption. Issues here involve ethically questionable sales techniques, reinforcing gender stereotypes, the creation of artificial wants and the targeting of vulnerable consumers (Crane & Matten, 2010).

A notorious case of questionable sales techniques involved so-called *beer girls* in Cambodia where young women represent and promote certain beer brands in local pubs. More than 75% of these women regularly and systematically supplement their income with paid sex. Breweries have been rather reticent in countering these practices (Marshall & Stecklow, 2000), and these women are at significantly increased risk for HIV (Kim et al., 2005).

Another issue is marketing strategies that support or promote gender stereotypes. There is evidence that the alcohol industry is quite strongly dependent on using sexual imagery in its advertisements to obtain consumer attention (Solomon, Ashmore, & Longo, 1992). Nevertheless, there seems to be little evidence that alcohol marketing campaigns provide unacceptably stereotypical pictures of gender differences. Ads for washing detergents, pizzas and instant dry soups and sauce mixes, to name a few, portrait men and women in far more stereotypical fashion. In fact, the conscious decision of marketers to treat men and women equally as potential consumers of alcohol and tobacco from the 1920s onwards may well have made several stereotypes disappear – the stereotype that it is only men who smoke and drink among them (Warsh, 1999). This development continues in a recent ad in Kenya in which three independent-looking urban and trendy women in a bar reject a man offering them a beer and take a Snapp, a new apple flavoured alcoholic beverage.

This brings us to what is arguably the most important ethical issue in marketing, and one largely overlooked in the ethics literature. It involves *alcopops* (flavoured alcoholic beverages also called ready-to-drink beverages or *malternatives*) such as Smirnoff Ice and Bacardi Breezer that provide young consumers, in particular women, with a sweet alternative to beer. Such alternatives had been available already before – think about ciders, sweet wines, flavoured beers, etc. – but these were hardly seen as premium products, did not typically feature tastes such as 'grand melón', 'black razz', 'torched cherry', 'peach red' or 'wolf berry', were not sold in cans hardly distinguishable from soft drinks, and unlike the alcopops, had a clear alcoholic taste. Marketing alcopops, Diageo (of Smirnoff) and Anheuser-Busch (of Bacardi) were very successful, combining as they did a premium brand name and a 'hard liquor image' with something sweet that does not taste like alcohol, and which is sold in supermarkets because it is classified – and taxed – as beer. This may have artificially created new desires for novel products. But even though some authors consider the creation of artificial desires as ethically problematic (Galbraith, 1974), I believe that it is very difficult to argue that there is something inherently wrong with designing a new kind of alcoholic drink.

Alcopops are, however, ethically problematic for a different reason which has to do with the phenomenon of *target marketing*. Market segmentation is an important contemporary marketing strategy, aiming as it does at finding significant and relevant differences between consumers and targeting one's products to particular sufficiently similar segments. As Smith and Cooper-Martin (1997) observe, when the segment contains *vulnerable* consumers and/or when the products are seen as *harmful*, an ordinarily acceptable marketing strategy may become unethical.

It is widely accepted among marketers that children and young adults are generally vulnerable consumers on the grounds that they lack capacity for full rational decision-making (Mazis, Ringold, Perry, & Denman, 1992), and the same applies to the elderly, people who are mentally ill and others. There is overwhelming evidence that non-targeted, general alcohol marketing contributes to underage drinking. Watching alcohol commercials on television, exposure to ads in magazines, exposure to displays of alcoholic beverages in supermarkets and other stores, possession of alcohol merchandise (key rings, wallets) and alcohol consumption in films are all correlated with early initiation of alcohol consumption (Anderson, de Bruijn, Angus, Gordon, & Hastings, 2009). Yet in the business ethics literature, the claim seems not to have been defended yet that the marketing of alcopops constitutes an unethical form of targeted marketing. Rather, attention has been restricted to the targeted marketing of particular alcohol beverages to racial minorities (Smith & Cooper-Martin, 1997).

Even though research on alcopops is rather scant, a number of important findings underscore my claim that alcopops form an important ethical challenge to the industry. First of all, underage drinkers are a very significant source of revenue for the alcohol industry. A US study estimated that underage drinkers (12–20 years) consume about 20% of the total number of drinks consumed (Foster, Vaughan, Foster, & Califano, 2003). By itself, this is no evidence of targeted marketing. But as Hughes et al. (1997) already indicate, alcopops are particularly attractive to consumers inexperienced with the taste of alcohol because the flavouring hides the taste of alcohol. Smirnoff Ice, for instance, just tastes like a variant of bitter lemon, the soft drink.

'The beauty of this category [of beverages] is that it brings in new drinkers, people who really don't like the taste of beer', said Marlene Coulis, spokeswoman of Anheuser-Busch, the producer of two bestselling alcopops, Bacardi Silver and Bacardi Breezer (Chura, 2002). And indeed, a study among Swiss children aged 13–16 years revealed that alcopops are often consumed in addition to other alcoholic drinks rather than replacing them. One research report from Brewing Research argued that 'along with lager, [alcopops] are the launching pad for most young people's drinking career' (Sharpe 2003 cited by Babor, 2009). This is underscored by studies about taste development showing that earlier exposure to certain tastes raises the likelihood that similar tastes will be accepted later on. In other words, alcopops diminish the 'natural barrier of the strong and often unpleasant taste of alcohol against experimentation' (Copeland, Stevenson, Gates, & Dillon, 2007). Moreover, there is some evidence that certain brewers and distillers actively perform marketing research among 15–17 year olds (Hastings et al., 2010).

Public goods, religious values and ethical issues

The most serious ethical issues in the alcohol industry, then, concern the marketing of alcoholic beverages. SRI investors are mostly tacit about their reasons for negatively screening alcohol. Is it these concerns that they implicitly use in their deliberation? In this section, I shall argue that the answer is very likely to be negative. Rather, if questioned, SRI investors will probably use an argument based on public goods, or an argument based on religious values. I shall introduce both arguments, and show that the Public Goods Argument is flawed and that the Religious Values Argument has limited scope in a world in which the bulk of shares is held by institutional rather than individual investors. I shall also argue that the Ethical Issues Argument has more to recommend, but that it does not succeed in defending a complete negative screen.

In abstract terms, the Public Goods Argument can be found in the writings of authors such as Kurtz (2009) and Lydenberg (2005). The starting point of this argument is what the Austrian economist Joseph Schumpeter called the *Adam Smith Problem* (Kurtz, 2009). One horn of the dilemma is formed by the morality of Smith's time emphasising the importance of altruism, benevolence and other moral norms and values. The other horn is inspired by the views of theorists such as Mandeville and Hobbes, and amounts to the view that it is egoism and self-interest that motivate our actions. The Adam Smith Problem, then, is whether we should be altruists or egoists.

One answer to this question is certainly Smith's invisible hand. Echoing Mandeville's maxim that private vices lead to public benefits, Smith's idea was that markets work best when egoistic individuals act in their own interests because an invisible hand will ensure the most efficient production of public goods. But this answer is typically invoked by *critics* of SRI to point out that SRI is based on a misunderstanding of how markets work. There is no need for SRI, the critics claim, because the actual market outcome is already the best possible world, resulting from individually egoistic activities leading to public benefits.

To show that there is a need for SRI nevertheless, Lydenberg (2005) provides an intricate argument to the effect that SRI is not only consistent with Smith's view of the invisible hand. More than that, he argues that Smith's views directly entail SRI. Lydenberg (2005) observes that unlike Mandeville, Smith was not against economic regulation and believed that society would be best served if individuals were led by virtuous self-interest. The invisible hand needs a bit of help.

What kind of help? Lydenberg (2005) proffers a very interesting suggestion to the effect that it is the stakeholders of a corporation – and in particular, its investors and consumers – that have to help the invisible hand. Slightly hyperbolically, Lydenberg (2005) claims that it is these stakeholders that *constitute* the invisible hand, 'steering' corporations as they do 'towards the public interest' (p. 107). The idea is that while businesspeople themselves will indeed merely be guided by egoism and self-interest and have no intention of promoting public goods, their egoism is offset by the actions of investors and stakeholders forcing these businesspeople to act in ways that promote the public good. Let us call this argument the Public Goods Argument.

The Public Goods Argument allegedly proffers an answer to the Adam Smith Problem. But used in the way SRI advocates use it, the Adam Smith Problem is a false dilemma because it is based on a dubious implicit assumption to the effect that corporations should be – and can be – genuinely concerned with public goods. Briefly and generally, my argument for this claim is twofold. First, what is a public good in a particular society is often a contested issue, and it is generally to be preferred that democratic decision-making procedures determine what public goods are. Leaving such decisions to stakeholder groups consisting of investors and consumers risks diminishing democratic legitimacy, in particular, in a world in which around 70% of the shares are owned by institutional rather than individual investors. Let us call this the problem of *legitimacy*. Second, in cases where the generation of public goods involves concerted actions from many sorts of actors besides corporations, investors and consumers, SRI strategies will fail to have the desired consequences. This is a problem of *effectiveness*.

The alcohol industry provides a good example of both legitimacy issues and effectiveness issues. It is beyond any doubt that alcohol abuse constitutes a massive health issue, and many countries have adopted tactics such as excise taxes, licensing laws, advertising restrictions, minimum purchasing age, maximum traveller import allowances, education and public information – or restricted sales by means such as the Swedish *systembolaget*. But few countries have banned the production, sales and consumption of alcohol altogether, and even if they have banned it, the primary motivation seems to have been grounded in religious concerns rather than in concerns about public health. Rather than embracing a Public Goods Argument, Islamic investors, for instance, exclude alcohol on the basis of private religious motives; they employ the Religious Values Argument.

In most countries, no democratic legitimacy will be obtained for complete prohibition, and this means that it is misleading, if not plain false, for an SRI fund with a negative screen on alcohol to defend the screen by reference to public goods or public interests. Rather than contributing to a public good, investors deciding not to invest in breweries, distilleries or companies that produce whisky bottles contribute to a world in which no alcohol is being produced at all. Such a world, however, is not seen as realising a public good in most democracies, and hence the Public Goods Argument is unsuccessful in defending a negative screen on alcohol.

The second problem of the Public Goods Argument lies in its assumption that when investors and consumers 'steer' the corporation, the self-interested behaviour of the corporations (or its directors, managers and employees) will lead to public benefits. This is not generally true. To foster public goods, corporations have to act together with government and with consumers (and other stakeholders), and often they will only do so if they are so forced by law. Public goods need coordinated action. To see this, suppose for the sake of argument that decreasing the number of alcohol-related deaths is a public good. Studies show that price regulation of alcoholic beverages is a very effective way to reduce mortality related to alcohol. But it would be perverse to ask the stakeholders singled out by Lydenberg (2005) – investors and consumers – to 'steer' a particular brewery or bottle factory into raising its prices, as this would put the company at competitive disadvantage. If democratic support can be obtained for intervention with the pricing of alcoholic beverages in order to contribute to the public good of decreasing alcohol-related mortality, considerations of justice require that such intervention ought to maintain a level playing field for all players in the alcohol industry. Consequently, it will have to be the result of government intervention (by means of excise taxes, for instance) or from self-regulation of the entire industry, and not only one company.

The failure of the Public Goods Argument to defend a negative screen on alcohol does not exclude an individual investor from having good personal reasons to withdraw from the alcohol industry altogether, and this brings us to the Religious Values Argument. Just like the vegetarian not buying shares in the meat industry, Islamic investors will not want to own alcohol shares, and a similar line of argumentation was uncovered in Wesley's sermon. Even though individual investors can consistently use this argument to defend completely ignoring the alcohol industry, institutional investors have to exercise more care. As long as individual investors can voluntarily select a fund, and the fund is explicit about its screens, there is nothing morally objectionable about the fund using religious values to back their selection criteria. But if the relation between the individual and the institutional investor is not voluntary (this is the case with many pension funds, healthcare plans, etc.), religious convictions of the institutional investor are forced upon individuals with potentially different religious views – or none at all. As a result, the Religious Value Argument is only a valid defence of a negative screen on alcohol for funds which can be freely chosen by people accepting the religious values the fund stands for.

Summarising the discussion so far, the Public Goods Argument is flawed because of problems of legitimacy and effectiveness, and the Religious Values Argument is unconvincing if it forces particular religious views on others. A more promising argument, therefore, is the Ethical Issues Argument. Just like investors adopting the Religious Values Argument, investors adopting this argument avoid speaking about public goods or interests. But unlike the Religious Values Argument, the Ethical Issues Argument is used by investors who are concerned with particular ethical issues in particular companies, and it is based on moral norms that these investors have good reasons to assume to be sufficiently universally accepted. An investor may, for instance, become convinced that target marketing of alcopops to children and young adolescents is unethical because of the fact that they cannot be considered to be fully rational decision-makers, expecting that a special concern for children would receive fairly universal support.

The Ethical Issues Argument is not an argument that can be used to defend a complete negative screen against the alcohol industry. Rather, the argument is sensitive to the differences between various alcohol corporations and may as a result lead investors to reject particular companies for particular reasons. But it does not necessarily recommend the adoption of negative selection criteria. On the contrary, in the light of what transpires from economics research about sin stocks, the Ethical Issues Argument may well suggest a larger role for advocacy campaigning, and a smaller role for SRI.

This literature reveals that if sufficiently many investors evade a particular industry, the cost of capital for that industry increases. Simplistically put, there is less demand for its shares, which means that investors are willing to pay less, and as a result, the corporation will get less. But if cost of capital increases, it is more expensive for a corporation to do what it wants to do – and what it should do from the perspective of ethics. This suggests that corporations with higher cost of capital will on average have less room to manoeuvre ethically, have to engage in more aggressive advertising, have fewer resources to spend on consumer information and education and so on. This is, to be clear, an empirical claim, and to my knowledge no research has been carried out to test it. But if it is true, it suggests that investors adopting the Ethical Issues Argument would rather abstain from using negative screens and opt for advocacy campaigning instead.

When large investors put a negative screen on alcohol they fail to take the opportunity to exercise their rights as shareholders and to change corporate strategy by means of advocacy campaigning. If shareholders leave a company as soon as it engages in activities they deem unethical, only those shareholder remain that see no wrong in the corporate strategy. Unless the number of retreating shareholders is so large as to leave the company under-funded, the effect may well be that the directors of the company never have to explicitly confront the issue. If negative selection criteria are used and no ethical investor remains shareholder, no shareholder will use the annual general meeting to voice ethical concerns about the issue; no lawsuits will be filed; and there will be no discussions with management about alternatives. The Ethical Issues Argument suggests that SRI funds should reconsider their negative screening against alcohol and try to obtain power as activist shareholders in alcohol corporations instead.

Conclusion

SRI is a booming business. But as I have argued in this article, the ethical arguments on which it rests are often shaky. While the alcohol industry was the first industry to be negatively screened by Methodist SRI investors *avant la lettre* in the eighteenth century using a Religious Values Argument, SRI investors nowadays mostly seem to adopt a Public Goods Argument, at least implicitly. I showed that this argument suffers from problems about democratic legitimacy and the effectiveness. Alcohol does constitute a massive health problem to a significant number of people, contributing around 2.3 million deaths a year worldwide. But overweight and obesity contribute 2.8 million deaths a year and physical inactivity 3.2 million. The fast food industry or the automobile industry are, however, hardly ever considered *sin stocks* in the literature, and positive screens for healthy food and the physical activities industry are exceedingly rare. It should, however, largely be left to democratic processes to determine the prioritisation of the concomitant public goods and the ways of reaching them.

I argued, however, that the Ethical Issues Argument can sensibly be used to justify some form of SRI. If investors have good reasons to doubt the morality of marketing strategies involving *beer girls* or of target marketing to under-aged individuals of *alcopops* such as Smirnoff Ice and Bacardi Breezer, then companies using these strategies could be divested.

But it is important to see that the Ethical Issues Argument does not force this form of shareholder democracy upon investors. As I indicated at several junctures in the article, more economics and finance research about the alcohol industry is needed. But the current state of the literature does suggest that when the alcohol industry is left to investors who do not care about ethics at all, we may be even further away from home ethically speaking.

Notes

1. In 2010, only screens on tobacco and Sudan were larger than screens on alcohol in terms of fund size. But Sudan is probably a temporary screen particularly by education endowments in the USA inspired by student and civic protesters concerned with the Darfur conflict (Social Investment Forum Foundation, 2010).
2. Anna Kajumulo Tibaijuka, Under-Secretary-General, United Nations Executive Director,UN-HABITAT, speech 11 February 2003, http://ww2.unhabitat.org/director/unf.asp (accessed 26 July 2012).

References

Anderson, D., Frost, G., Hodgson, P., Minogue, K., O'Hear, A., & Scruton, R. (1996). *What has 'ethical investment' to do with ethics?* London: Social Affairs Unit.

Anderson, P., de Bruijn, A., Angus, K., Gordon, R., & Hastings, G. (2009). Impact of alcohol advertising and media exposure on adolescent alcohol use: A systematic review of longitudinal studies. *Alcohol and Alcoholism*, *44*, 229–243.

Babor, T. F. (2009). Alcohol policy, academic medicine and the alcoholic beverage industry. Conference on Industry-Medicine Relationships: Comparing Tobacco, Alcohol, Food and Pharmaceuticals, New York.

Babor, T. F., Edwards, G., & Stockwell, T. (1996). Science and the drinks industry: Cause for concern. *Addiction*, *91*, 5–9.

Bekelman, J.E., Li, Y., & Gross, C.P. (2003). Scope and impact of financial conflicts of interest in biomedical research: A systematic review. *Journal of the American Medical Association, 289*(4), 454–465.

Chura, H. (2002, 22 April). Beer marketing: Brewers binge on malt drinks. *Advertising Age, 73*(16), p. 60.

Copeland, J., Stevenson, R. J., Gates, P., & Dillon, P. (2007). Young Australians and alcohol: The acceptability of ready-to-drink (RTD) alcoholic beverages among 12–30-year-olds. *Addiction*, *102*, 1740–1746.

Cowton, C. J. (1994). The development of ethical investment products. In A. R. Prindl & B. Prodhan (Eds.), *Ethical conflicts in finance* (pp. 213–232). Oxford: Oxford University Press.

Cowton, C. J. (1999). Playing by the rules: Ethical criteria at an ethical investment fund. *Business Ethics: A European Review*, *8*, 60–69.

Crane, A., & Matten, D. (2010). *Business ethics: Managing corporate citizenship in the age of globalization.* Oxford: Oxford University Press.

El Ghoul, S., Guedhami, O., Kwok, C. C. Y., & Mishra, D. R. (2011). Does corporate social responsibility affect the cost of capital? *Journal of Banking and Finance*, *35*, 2388–2406.

Foster, S. E., Vaughan, R. D., Foster, W. H., & Califano, J. A. Jr. (2003). Alcohol consumption and expenditures for underage drinking and adult excessive drinking. *Journal of the American Medical Association*, *289*, 989–995.

Galbraith, J. K. (1974). *The new industrial state.* Harmondsworth: Penguin.

Godfrey, C. (2004). The financial costs and benefits of alcohol, *The Globe*. Retrieved July 26, 2012, from http://www.ias.org.uk/resources/publications/theglobe/globe200401-02/gl200401-02_p7.html

Hastings, G., Brooks, O., Stead, M., Angus, K., Anker, T., & Farrell, T. (2010). Alcohol advertising: The last chance saloon. *British Medical Journal, 340*, 184–186.

Heineken. (2012). *Heineken sustainability report.* Amsterdam: Author.

Hong, H., & Kacperczyk, M. (2009). The price of sin: The effects of social norms on markets. *Journal of Financial Economics, 93*, 15–36.

Hughes, K., MacKintosh, A. M., Hastings, G., Wheeler, C., Watson, J., & Inglis, J. (1997). Young people, alcohol, and designer drinks: Quantitative and qualitative study. *British Medical Journal, 314*, 414–418.

Kim, A. A., Sun, L. P., Chhorvann, C., Lindan, C., Van Griensven, F., Kilmarx, P. H., . . ., & Page-Shafer, K. (2005). High prevalence of HIV and sexually transmitted infections among indirect sex workers in Cambodia. *Sexually Transmitted Diseases, 32*, 745–751.

Kurtz, L. (2009). Socially responsible investment and shareholder activism. In A. Crane, A. McWilliams, D. Matten, J. Moon, & D. S. Siegel (Eds.), *The Oxford handbook of corporate social responsibility* (pp. 249–280). Oxford: Oxford University Press.

Leoywanichjalearn, Y. (2012). Cost-benefit analysis of listing thai beverage company: The case study of unethical stock in Thailand. *Asian Securities and Investment Federation eJournal, 12*, 2012.

Louche, C., & Lydenberg, S. (2010). Responsible investing. In J. Boatright (Ed.), *Finance ethics: Critical issues in theory and practice* (pp. 393–417). Hoboken, NJ: Wiley.

Lydenberg, S. (2005). *Corporations and the public interest: Guiding the invisible hand.* San Francisco: Berrett-Koehler.

Mackenzie, C. (1998). The choice of criteria in ethical investment. *Business Ethics: A European Review, 7*, 81–86.

Marshall, S., & Stecklow, S. (2000, 31 May). Cambodia's 'beer girls' peddle the product and endure the hassle. *Wall Street Journal Eastern Edition, 235*(107), pA1.

Matzopoulos, R., Parry, C. D., Corrigall, J., Myers, J., Goldstein, S., & London, L. (2012). Global Fund collusion with liquor giant is a clear conflict of interest. *Bulletin World Health Organization, 90*, 67–69.

Mazis, M. B., Ringold, D. J., Perry, E. S., & Denman, D. W. (1992). Perceived age and attractiveness of models in cigarette advertisements. *Journal of Marketing, 56*, 22–37.

Monks, R. A. G., & Minow, N. (2004). *Corporate governance.* Malden: Blackwell.

O'Rourke, A. (2003). A new politics of engagement: Shareholder activism for corporate social responsibility. *Business Strategy and the Environment, 12*, 227–239.

Parkinson, J. E. (1993). *Corporate power and responsibility.* Oxford: Oxford University Press.

Peele, S. (2000). Exploring psychological benefits associated with moderate alcohol use: A necessary corrective to assessments of drinking outcomes? *Drug and Alcohol Dependence, 60*, 221–247.

Salaber, J. M. (2009). *The determinants of sin stock returns: Evidence on the European market*, working paper. Retrieved July 26, 2012, from http://papers.ssrn.com/sol3/papers.cfm?abstract_id=1071746

SAM Sustainability Investing. (2012). *The sustainability yearbook.* Zurich: Author.

Smith, N.C., & Cooper-Martin, E. (1997). Ethics and target marketing: The role of product harm and consumer vulnerability. *Journal of Marketing, 61*, 1–20.

Social Investment Forum Foundation. (2010). *Report on socially responsible investment trends in the United States.* Washington: Author.

Solomon, M. R., Ashmore, R. D., & Longo, L. C. (1992). Congruence between types of beauty and product images in advertising. *Journal of Advertising, 21*, 23–34.

Sparkes, R. (2001). Ethical investment: Whose ethics, which investment? *Business Ethics: A European Review, 10*, 194–205.

Warsh, C. K. (1999). Smoke and mirrors: Gender representation in North American tobacco and alcohol advertisements before 1950. *Histoire Sociale: Social History, 32*, 183–222.

Wine and Spirit Trade Association. (2012). *UK wine and spirit market overview.* London: Author.

World Health Organization. (2011). *Global status report on alcohol and health.* Geneva: Author.

Two decades and a Category 5 hurricane later . . . tracking homeless substance abusers in New Orleans

Rachel L. Rayburn

Department of Public Policy, Indiana University–Purdue University Fort Wayne, Fort Wayne, IN, USA

This paper outlines the qualitative methods utilised in a long-term follow-up study of a non-traditional population: homeless substance abusers in New Orleans. The purpose of this research project was to identify possible desistance variables in the lives of homeless substance abusers and estimate their effects on various life outcomes. By way of phone, mail and in-person interviews, this research examines the life course of a sample of New Orleans homeless substance abusers from the time they entered into treatment (1991) until the present and observes the quality of their social bonds and their long-term outcomes. By making use of longitudinal research methods, this project gives a more thorough understanding of homelessness and substance abuse.

Many of the questions that social scientists are interested in answering about homeless substance abusers are best addressed by collecting data on the same people over time. The use of these long-term collections in studies of homeless substance abusers has been minimal, but contacting homeless substance abusers over time is a vital methodological issue. The full assessment of the success of substance abuse treatment and transitional housing interventions requires a longitudinal research design, a long time frame and a large sample.

The average response rate in substance abuse studies of non-homeless populations is approximately 75%, with a range from 34% to 95% (Biglan et al., 1997). Because there are so few studies of homeless substance abusers over time, we cannot speculate on the average response rate for this group. It would be fair to say that they would generally be much lower. Locating the subjects for follow-up interviews and encouraging respondent cooperation are major impediments to collecting longitudinal data (Thornton, Freedman, & Camburn, 1982).

The trials and successes of longitudinal research designs among many types of projects are helpful for other researchers embarking on this type of research. For the current follow-up study, I tracked homeless substance abusers in New Orleans over the course of nearly two decades. The main barriers to this type of research design included inexperience with tracking those without stable addresses, the destruction caused by Hurricane Katrina and cost.

The main determinants of success in tracking individuals are the size, mobility and dispersion of the sample, the amount of time that has elapsed between follow-ups, and the persistence and creativity of investigators (Clarridge, Sheehy, & Hauser, 1978). For this project, I set out knowing that many of these factors were stacked against me. The initial sample was fairly large (670), but homeless individuals are known to frequently be unstably housed, and Katrina devastated New

Orleans in 2005. Further, approximately 18–19 years had passed since any contact was established with the sample. As I set out to track these individuals, I knew I must be especially persistent and creative to compensate. Eckland (1968) supports this method, expressing that persistence with prodding is much more important than finding the correct type of prodding device.

However, perseverance alone would not enable me to find these individuals. The research methodology for the follow-up interviews was much more of a craft than a science (Clarridge et al., 1978). To achieve any valuable response from this sample, I took a multi-faceted tracking approach (Wright & Devine, 1995). An intrinsic problem with follow-up studies is that the research conclusions could be biased because of the selective attrition of respondents. In other words, data are based on who is willing and able to respond, and who is willing and able to respond is dependent upon a variety of factors in this population. When I set out to find these homeless substance abusers, I realised that the ones I would find would most likely be the success stories and I would most likely be able to find the ones who had addresses or telephones. The individuals who have addresses that are housed ('the successes') greatly differ from those I was not able to find.

This paper outlines the original programme, its purpose and a description of the participants. It then moves on to describe research methods utilised including mail follow-up, phone tracking, field tracking, agency participation in locating individuals and Internet tracking. The successes and failures of each method are described, along with a sample of what type of qualitative data were collected. The costs of this follow-up study are explained and the differences between the original sample and those contacted years later examined. The limitations of this project are explained, and suggestions for future research using a longitudinal design are given.

Programme description

The New Orleans Homeless Substance Abusers Program (NOHSAP) was a residentially based, adult resocialisation project for homeless alcoholics and drug abusers in the greater New Orleans area. NOHSAP was designed to attain four goals: (1) sobriety from drugs and alcohol, (2) stable housing, (3) economic independence and (4) a reduction in family estrangement. By way of well-designed interventions, NOHSAP hoped to reintegrate homeless substance abusers into society. The philosophy for NOHSAP was that until secure housing was taken care of, homeless individuals would have little chance of conquering their alcohol and drug problems. NOHSAP was based on a social learning perspective: just as individuals learn to use substances, they can learn new ones. NOHSAP was an experimental programme based on the idea that there is hope for even the most incapacitated among the homeless.

NOHSAP was designed as an intervention with three phases: (1) detoxification, (2) transitional care and (3) independent living. The process of detoxification was designed as a 7-day programme of getting off substances, being introduced to Alcoholics Anonymous (AA) and Narcotics Anonymous (NA) meetings, and counselling and meeting with a case manager. Both individual and family detoxification facilities were available, with a 40-bed capacity. NOHSAP was the only treatment facility in Louisiana, and possibly in the Southeast, where women could come with children and still receive full treatment services when created.

Transitional care, following detoxification, consisted of a 21-day programme with only 12 beds. Assessment was much more thorough, group meetings were held twice a day and clients attended off-site AA and NA meetings. Individuals who completed this transitional phase became eligible for the 20-bed, 12-month Independent Living programme. All of the same services within transitional care were still present, but services such as job training and placement and education (GED (General Educational Development tests)) were added. There were no charges associated with living in any of these phases of the programme.

Description of participants

The clients overwhelmingly comprised African-Americans (82%). The average age at the time of entry was 32 years. About one-third of the men were veterans of the armed forces. Most of the clients had some work history and some job skills at the time the programme started, but as a whole, they were not prepared for long-term employment. Most of the clients had limited educational backgrounds, but the majority had at least a high school diploma. The vast majority were New Orleanian, born and raised in the city.

Most were experiencing their first episode of homelessness when they entered NOHSAP. The clients for NOHSAP were generally recruited at the Charity Hospital Emergency Room. Over half of the clients (53%) identified themselves as multiple substance abusers, slightly less than half (48%) reported having problems with alcohol and a very large percentage (85%) reported abusing crack cocaine. Prior to NOHSAP, about one-quarter had previously gone through some sort of alcohol treatment programme and about double that had gone through drug treatment.

At the start of the present follow-up study in 2010, the average age of the NOHSAP client was 51 years. The oldest original subject is currently 86 years of age and the youngest 36 years. When designing the questionnaires and interview schedules for NOHSAP, the original researchers put emphasis on follow-up interviews, as they expected to track these individuals as long as possible. The last 15–20 min of the interviews was devoted to obtaining information on where the client normally spends time, emergency contact information, mailing addresses, presence of visible tattoos and aliases (street names). However, after two decades, most of this information proved to be irrelevant in finding these individuals. The researchers on the original New Orleans Homeless Substance Abusers Project stressed each individual's motivation to participate. The clients from the programme appreciated being part of something valuable and enjoyed having the opportunity to help others. The original staff (those who conducted the interviews) were trained to establish rapport with clients, which proved to be much more important in the follow-up process than any other identifying information.

Mail follow-up

Contact by mail is one of the least expensive tracking methods available, and perhaps the least amount of effort and training is required. Therefore, sending a letter on a university letterhead was the first method of contacting NOHSAP clients. To rely upon mailed letters is to assume that the respondent both has and uses a mailing address. Current addresses were mainly obtained using ZabaSearch.com and Intelius.com. About 60% of the initial mail-outs were returned as non-deliverable. As for the letters that were delivered, it is a guess as to how many actually ended up in the hands of former NOHSAP clients.

When trying to contact respondents, follow-up letters were personalised as much as possible. The first class letter on the university letterhead thanked them for being part of the original study and asked them for being reinterviewed at their convenience. The inside address of the letters included a 'Dear Mr' or 'Dear Ms' salutation and a blue ballpoint pen signature at the bottom. During the first set of mailings, the respondents were sent a stamped self-addressed envelope to mail back their whereabouts, perhaps by including a phone number. In addition to this envelope, two $1 bills were included. However, no client used the return envelope, and about half of the letters in the first mailing were returned as undeliverable. Successive mailings without these two inclusions indicate that these inclusions had no noticeable effect on the response rate.

Over the course of this project, a total of 1010 letters were sent to addresses thought to be held by former NOHSAP clients. Of these, half were sent back as undeliverable (507 letters, 50.2%). At 33.5 cents a letter, the cost of the mailings totalled $338. Mailings were sent out in increments, about 50 letters at a time. Over the course of the 16 mailings, small changes were implemented, which seemed to have no effect on the response rate. Spending more time personalising the letters and including two $1 bills had no effect on the response rate. If individuals felt that it was important to participate in a follow-up study, they called. The types of individuals who responded to my letters were in most cases successes. Individuals living on the streets, or in shelters, did not receive my letters. Finding these individuals required travelling to New Orleans and close contact with the homeless shelters, prisons and treatment centres in the area.

The first letter

Within a week of mailing the letters, 24 came back as undeliverable, but one man from Huntsville, AL, called my office. As the letters came back, I felt frustrated, but not surprised. I figured that at least half of the letters had made it to someone and that I would be hearing back from more people shortly. After 3 months, only the one individual from Huntsville had responded. The first mailing served as a pilot study of sorts; I examined methods to determine how the response rate could be improved.

Hope for the follow-up study remained with a successful interview with Chris, a white male living in Huntsville, AL. Chris called my office as soon as he got the letter, late on a weeknight. Normally I would not have been in my office, but was working extra hours on this project. Surprised that the phone rang, I picked it up and Chris asked for me. After confirming that he reached the right number, he asked 'How did you find me?'.

This question made me very nervous. I knew that there was a good possibility that many of these individuals had a strong desire to NOT to be contacted, but was unprepared for it to be happening. After a few minutes of talking, I realised that Chris was just surprised, happy to talk with me, not upset that I contacted him. In fact, on the next day, I found two messages from him on the department voicemail. Due to my surprise, I did not feel prepared to conduct the interview on the spot. I grabbed a nearby notepad and began writing down everything that I could. I asked for contact information and a good time to call back and set up an interview for the following evening.

By the time this interview opportunity came up, I had a good idea of what I wanted to find out. After several rounds with the Institutional Review Board (IRB), a list of question protocols emerged. However, I did not have any idea of how the questions or process would actually culminate. Feeling that I sacrificed some of the depth of the project to meet the IRB requirements, I was curious as to how much information the respondents would give to the questions that had been approved. Further, I only had a vague idea of what to ask these individuals. What I thought were important, relevant questions to ask a homeless substance abuser 18 years later might be completely irrelevant.

The original data set was in essence a life-history questionnaire. Pages of information up until 1991 including many aspects of these individuals' lives had been documented. It only made sense to start asking them questions about incidents that took place after the 1991 interview. However, it was difficult for Chris to open up and talk to me just starting from 1991. His life story ran together and he was often telling me stories that preceded this date. For example, I hypothesised that types of employment held by these individuals would be a key factor in keeping them housed and sober, so I asked 'What type of employment have you held since 1991?' Luckily, Chris had been working the same job for many years. If constructing this follow-up questionnaire again, I would ask 'Tell me about your current job,' followed by 'Tell me about your job before that.' This way we could work backwards, a much easier task than recalling where you were 18 years ago.

On the following evening, I called Chris and we talked extensively (58 min) about his life since 1991. He felt that he was very lucky that he wound up with his current employer and that he could work his way up through the ranks to have a fairly respectable career. The same experience following my inquiry about employment occurred when I asked him about his marriage. 'Are you currently married?' He replied yes and I followed with 'Tell me about your past marital history over the last eighteen years.' Chris told that he had only been married to one woman during the 18 years, a commitment which he credits with getting him out of homelessness. He was able to tell me the story about how they started dating while he was living at the homeless shelter and their subsequent marriage. With multiple marriages, however, this question may have caused confusion.

Chris answered several other similar questions about children, arrests, hospitalisations and homelessness. The interview went extremely smoothly, yet I missed not sitting in front of him and examining his facial expressions. Chris wanted to show me pictures of his children and wife and could only do so through email. He wanted to show me his home and his work which he so proudly obtained.

One concern arose at the end of the interview with Chris; he asked to be my Facebook friend. He said that he wanted to be friends so that he could show me pictures of his family and keep in contact. This was very surprising and had never occurred in any other interview that I conducted previously, and I did not know exactly how to respond. Pausing for some consideration, I decided to add him as a friend, but kept all personal information on a strict privacy setting. When conducting multi-modal interviews in this age of increased technology, precautions and thought should be given to the issue of social networking.

Despite the disadvantages of the phone interview, advantages included not having to show compassionate facial expressions, enabling me to write seven pages of notes. This first interview on the phone went by quickly; there was a large amount of rapid dialogue going back and forth. People at both ends of the phone line probably felt a little uncomfortable and spoke quickly to fill awkward gaps in the conversation. Generally, with face-to-face interviews, there seems to be more pause between thoughts. This first interview with Chris was a benchmark; it gave me an idea of what to expect from the remainder of the 31 interviews to be conducted.

Phone tracking

For about a quarter of the sample, at least one phone number was obtained through the previously mentioned search engines used to locate the mailing addresses. Prior research indicates that telephone contacts yield higher response rates than mail contacts (Alwin and Jensen cited in Clarridge et al., 1978, p. 189). Generally, interest and enthusiasm can be conveyed much more readily in spoken words than in printed words. Also, telephones allow one to eliminate or pursue a follow-up interview much more quickly than mail. However, in this population, every phone number obtained proved to be either unserviceable or a wrong number. Therefore, mailing was a much more reliable method of tracking than telephone calls. Perhaps with more people using cellphones, and these numbers generally unavailable for specific searches, this method is increasingly dated to the point of hopelessness.

Agency tracking

Some follow-up success in previous studies has been found from referral agencies (Eckland, 1968, p. 60), such as non-profit service providers. In August 2010, I made my first trip to New Orleans as a researcher. I had two goals upon arriving during the 3-day trip: (1) to have a meeting with Bridge House, a local homeless and substance abuse facility, and (2) to visit some of the addresses where letters had not been returned to inquire as to why no one had responded.

The process of looking through the records of 670 individuals through the Bridge House records was nearly impossible. Bridge House has limited resources and assigned me to work with two employees who could help me with the records. Unfortunately, I could not sit down with the system by myself; I had to have someone doing the work for me. Looking through all 670 files would have taken a full day, if not two. Therefore, I decided to take the first three pages of files (138 individuals) and spend a few hours looking their information up. The specific job of these two employees was to conduct follow-up interviews for Bridge House clients up to a year after their graduation from the programme. Initially, the employees were hesitant to spend time helping me. They said that they had difficulty in keeping up with the follow-up interviews after 3 months and asked how I expected to find the same individuals nearly 20 years later. I explained how important the project was and that I had travelled to New Orleans to try. They were impressed by my persistence and agreed to help.

Unfortunately, none of the 138 NOHSAP clients were currently receiving treatment at Bridge House, but 12 had gone through the facility after NOHSAP. That means that about 9% of NOHSAP individuals received drug and alcohol treatment at Bridge House after NOHSAP. Some individuals came in immediately after NOHSAP (August 1993) and some were there much more recently (September 2004). Some individuals were even at Bridge House before and after NOHSAP (March 1990 and June 2000).

Looking through the files of Bridge House did not provide much assistance in the direct tracking of individuals. However, meeting employees who had the same follow-up goals and were willing to help had enormous dividends. Both individuals were willing to share resources, phone numbers and methods of follow-ups that I had not known about previously. Most importantly, one individual showed me how to use the Louisiana Department of Corrections (DOC) inmate tracker, which became imperative to the success of this project.

Go directly to jail

In fact, the most effective way of tracking these individuals came from the Louisiana DOC Inmate Locator. This offender locator system is available to the public. By using a Touch-Tone phone, anyone can access the offender locator system 24 h a day. Callers need to know the offender's DOC number or may enter the offender's name and date of birth to access housing assignment, address of the facility where the offender is located, a contact phone number and a projected release date. The system is updated every 24 h and also includes information on those offenders under probation or parole.

With the first pass of the NOHSAP through the database, I was able to obtain confirmed addresses for 56 individuals. I learnt that five individuals were serving life sentences at the state penitentiary, and the others were divided, with half being on probation or parole and the other half serving sentences in various correctional centres around the state of Louisiana. I sent out letters to all of these individuals and the response rate was much higher among incarcerated individuals than what was observed in previous mailings. Within 2 weeks, nine incarcerated individuals responded to my request to interview them.

Incarcerated individuals were much more willing to agree to follow-up interviews. They were often desperate for attention, lonely and wanted someone to listen to them. Some of the incarcerated individuals never responded to the letters. Some responded once and never wrote again, and others are still writing letters. Many of the individuals wrote very long letters, almost always in difficult-to-read cursive lettering. Some sent Christmas and Valentine's Day cards wishing for happy holidays. They often inquired not about the study, but about the researcher. They asked questions about favourite movies, music, pets and personal relationships and sometimes requested pictures.

The longer a person was serving out a sentence, the more desire the person had to foster a relationship. The letters were often sad, depressing and utterly devoid of hope. One time, a letter came to the university addressed from a man who was never enrolled in NOHSAP. He was serving a life sentence at the state penitentiary and wrote a three-page letter asking for help. One of the five lifers must have given (or sold) him the information from the follow-up study. Another currently incarcerated NOHSAP client refused to participate in the follow-up study unless I met certain demands. The list of demands included things such as being transferred to another prison, soap, T-shirts and shoes. He explained that having these things would give him some reputation in the prison that he was currently lacking.

Most of the incarcerated individuals openly welcomed an in-person interview. Some asked about the specific day so that they could get a haircut and look presentable. When I got consent from several individuals that they would participate in a follow-up in-person interview, I began to write letters to the wardens of the prisons asking them where they were located. The majority of the wardens worked with me to ensure progress with the research project. Only on one occasion did a prison warden deny my request to conduct research. The warden of that prison said that my research provided no benefit to the institution and therefore I was not welcome to visit. Even after mailing a second letter explaining how this research could directly benefit the population and institution, I was denied.

After receiving approval from three prisons, I planned a trip to Baton Rouge, LA, to conduct face-to-face interviews with about a dozen incarcerated individuals. (For a full explanation of the costs associated with this project, see Appendix 1.) From the Baton Rouge airport, I rented a car and set up a base in St Francisville, Louisiana, about 30 miles north of the airport. St Francisville is a small town comprising mostly bed and breakfast inns and antique shops with a population of about 2000. The choice of lodging was primarily decided upon by a recommendation of an employee at the Louisiana State Penitentiary.

Getting settled in late, research started the following morning at the state penitentiary. The city of Angola is about 25 miles northwest of St Francisville, but the travel time is about 45 min figuring in bridges and possible stops. The drive through Tunica Hills to get to the prison is beautiful, as is the land upon which the penitentiary is located. It took about 40 min to get through security, as I had to be escorted by the warden's assistant at all times. From the assistant's office, we immediately went to start the interviews. Four of the five individuals serving life sentences were located in the same building; the fifth was on lockdown and required us to travel to another cellblock.

By the time the assistant and I got to the main dormitory-style facility, all four inmates were lined up outside waiting for us. All four were black men, wearing mostly denim attire so dated that it looked as if decades had passed. The assistant and I entered into a room with the first inmate who was cuffed on both the wrists and ankles. This individual had recently got into some trouble and many of his privileges had been taken away. After the interview, the warden's assistant scolded the inmate for the way he talked during my interview. The assistant said the inmate needed to stop blaming other people and expressed disappointment at his recent troubles.

The next two inmates originally refused to participate in the interview. They entered the room carrying many legal documents, clearly hoping to make a case to me to be released. Before I had a chance to explain that I could be of no assistance, they refused participation for another reason. The prison required individuals participating in research to sign a consent form. This form gave the prison the right to make determinations about the prisoner based on what was said during the interview. In other words, what was said during the interview could later come to cause problems for the individuals. The two individuals who originally refused to participate still had a great deal of hope that their cases could be appealed and did not want to do anything that could possibly jeopardise their chances of release.

After the interviews were completed, I was taken on a tour of the state penitentiary. The tour was rather extensive as the prison is located on 18,000 acres, with a little over 5000 inmates and

1800 staff members. We toured a small town inside the prison gates where some 200 employees live. Their children are picked up for school by buses and come back to the prison grounds after school. We may have spent the longest time visiting the dog kennels. Angola staff are especially proud of the dogs they breed. Trained dogs included Bloodhounds, German Shepherds, Rottweilers and wolves.

Also on the tour was the inmate cemetery. Most individuals who come to Angola never leave, and many bodies are never claimed or removed by relatives. Only recently has the prison started providing coffins for inmates (made by other inmates). The prison has also been training inmates in hospice care, so inmates are taking care of other inmates in their last hours at Angola (see Rayburn, Pals, & Wright, 2012 for more).

For lunch, we drove over to the warden's ranch house, where inmates prepared an extensive, traditional southern meal. Big Lew is the chef at the ranch house and gets help with the cooking from Samuel, ET and Hop Sing. Big Lew, in addition to cooking for the warden, at one time cooked for the Governor of Louisiana. Almost everything that we ate was grown on the 18,000 acres of the Louisiana State Penitentiary. Fresh mustard greens, corn, chicken, beef, mashed potatoes, gravy, corn bread, sweet iced tea, fresh chocolate chip cookies and lemon meringue pie were all on the menu that afternoon at the ranch house. Inmates insisted on pulling the chair out for me, bringing me everything, addressing me as ma'am, frequently refilling my drink and cleaning up everything immediately after I was finished.

Lunch was also a time to talk to a few guards about what I was doing there. As soon as I mentioned homelessness, sociology, desistance or anything about the project, they had an opportunity to ask pointed questions about the problem of recidivism. One guard's father had worked in Angola, and his brother now works there as well. He wanted to make sure that he educated me about left-leaning sociologists and their ridiculous conceptions about wanting to regulate firearms.

After lunch, I headed back to St Francisville. It was a long, very odd day at Angola. I did not find it nearly as dreary as I thought; in fact, the people treated me so nicely that I almost did not want to leave. Some have referred to Angola as a modern-day slave plantation. I felt this quite deeply during parts of the visit, especially during lunch. Angola, the largest prison in the USA, is the only prison with its own zip code. Inmates are predominately black men who participate in planting, picking cotton and taking care of crops. The visit was ironic: beautiful acres of land with the one purpose of incapacitating thousands of men for the rest of their lives.

On the second day of the trip, a very early start began my miniature road trip to Angie, LA. Four of the men from the original sample were incarcerated at Rayburn Correctional Center, some 100 miles east of my base. Angie is a town of about 250 and is situated on the Mississippi border. The wardens of Rayburn were especially welcoming of my visit to the prison. One of the wardens highly emphasised education among the inmates and was excited to have a scholar come to visit and conduct research.

The scenery of the 200-plus mile round trip drive to Angie was similar to that in Angola, with rolling hills, haystacks, horses and beautiful scenery. The interviews went well; I was allowed to sit with the inmates alone in an office with a shut door. Interviewees were much more open in answering questions in this environment and there was no pressure for speeding the interviews along, so the data collected were rich. At the end of the interviews, the assisting warden asked for my help. He asked for textbooks for inmates, my availability to teach courses for free and other institutional support. This put me in a rather difficult situation, as I felt indebted to the staff for all their assistance. I indicated that I would investigate providing what assistance I could. Like Chris' Facebook friending, this onsite situation is one that I had not planned when working with needy organisations or people. Future follow-up studies under similar circumstances should be prepared to offer what assistance is available, but also as to how to tactfully decline.

On the third day of the trip, I had a tight schedule as I had an evening flight to catch. The final prison stop, Dixon Correctional Institute, is a mere 15-min drive from St Francisville. I was scheduled to meet with four inmates, but upon arriving, I found that one had been released. I asked for information about the location of the offender, but was told that I would not receive any help finding him. The feel of this prison was completely different from that of the last two. It was obvious that I was not welcome from the minute I stepped onto the property. I was told to stand and wait for my escort at the prison gates. When the truck quickly pulled up and stopped, a strong hand on the horn was my pick up.

My escort had no desire to help me and did not want to hear anything about the research that I was conducting. For the first two interviews, I met inmates in a recreational meeting room. Generally, I was left alone, but staff came in and out throughout the interviews causing disruptions. For the third interview, I was taken to another building where I interviewed the third individual in an employee's office with the door open. Staff stood outside talking, working and generally handling the day-to-day operations of the prison. After the interview, I was promptly escorted off the property and instructed on how to get home.

Field tracking

On a separate trip from conducting the prison interviews, I flew to New Orleans to visit some of the addresses listed for NOHSAP clients. Finding NOHSAP clients by travelling to the listed addresses proved to be expensive, time consuming and generally pointless. On day 1, I picked five addresses that were close to my hotel in New Orleans. For two addresses, someone answered the door, looking very suspicious of me and indicated that no one by that name resided there. For another two addresses, no one answered the door and I left a printed letter similar to the one that I mailed initially. For the final address, I talked to a person's neighbour who indicated that someone by that name did in fact live there, and I left a printed letter on her door. I never heard from anyone at the addresses where these letters were left.

On day 2, I was very exhausted and disappointed in my lack of success the previous day, but set out nonetheless to visit four addresses. At the first address, no one answered the door, so I left a letter. At the second address, the client's mother answered the door and I talked with her for quite some time. She indicated that she did receive the original letter and forwarded it to her son. She told me that he evacuated to Dallas, TX, during Hurricane Katrina and never came back. She said that she would give him my contact information so that he could call me for an interview. She was very glad that I stopped by, insisted on hugging me and told me how lonely living in the lower ninth ward was since Katrina. She spent 5 years evacuated as her home was being rebuilt, but was now happy to live on the only piece of land that she has ever owned.

On the third stop, I met another family member of an NOSHAP client, but she was not nearly as delighted to see me. Sister to one of the clients, she replied to my inquiry by saying that 'he don't come around here no more'. With some prodding, she gave me his new address and sent me on my way. The final address was a law office, with no place to leave a letter, and most likely was just a mailing mistake.

Discussion

A number of variables were at work to make this project very interesting methodologically. Creativity was used to find ways to conduct these interviews and this made for a rather non-standard interview set. For example, due to the distance between myself and many of the incarcerated respondents, many pages of the interview data are in letters written between jails and the university. Some interviews were conducted in person in Louisiana ($n = 9$); the majority were

Table 1. Demographics of the original sample and follow-up.

	Original sample (%)	Follow-up (%)
Race (black)	78	82
Detox-only	76	78
Never married	56	72
Gender (male)	85	91

conducted by telephone ($n = 15$) and some by snail mail ($n = 8$). However, in many cases, a combination of one or two methods was used to collect as much information as possible.

For example, in some cases, letters were written before and after an in-person interview. Some individuals, after the telephone interview, wrote letters telling me that they wanted to be more open during the phone interview, but could not do so because someone was listening in another room. For these reasons, the standard set of interview questions became very unstructured. From the start of data collection to the end, 59 letters were received by individuals during the study. These are mostly what have been come to be known in the university mailroom as 'jail mail'. Incarcerated individuals understand the nature of this research project, but have little or no communication with the outside world. So, they continue to write and these letters are important sources about the life histories of the individuals from NOHSAP.

With all of these tracking methods utilised, I conducted interviews with 32 NOHSAP clients. The characteristics of the follow-up sample closely matched those of the original sample (Table 1). The percentage of never-married individuals in the follow-up sample was higher (72% compared with 56% of the original sample); this is most likely because of the high number of interviews conducted on incarcerated individuals. Similarly, 91% of the follow-up sample were male and only 9% were female. Again, this is most likely a characteristic of the incarceration rate. Another possibility is the higher likelihood of single men being more willing to talk to a female interviewer.

The 2-h interview that the individuals participated in during the original NOHSAP data collection was the longest sustained interaction some individuals had with a single individual in years. This rapport proved very useful, and in several of the follow-up interviews that I conducted, these individuals assumed that I was the original interviewer and asked me several specific questions. This follow-up study proved to be methodologically diverse, included successes and failures, and will hopefully be of use to others working in the field to track non-traditional populations.

Conclusion

Findings from the quantitative results of this study show that social bonding theory seems to be a weak explanation scheme in this population. The results from the qualitative data, however, are contrary and show social bonds to be crucial in the desistance process. Like what had been observed in Laub and Sampson's study, marriage and employment were strong predictors of desistance. Individuals who were interviewed tended to be sober, but disaffiliated with 12-step meetings. Other themes from the interviews involve the presentation of self, the importance of religion and a process of ageing out of crime.

Getting individuals away from the environment in which they are located, mentally and physically, seems to be important for desistance. This distancing was done in a few ways among the NOHSAP individuals, but seemed to be most powerful when a marriage was coupled with a residential move. Marriages are one of the most important components of life satisfaction and well-being throughout a person's life (Lucas & Dyrenforth, 2006; Waite & Gallagher, 2001). As human beings, we have built-in mechanisms to protect and foster committed relationships (Maner,

Gailliot, & Miller, 2009). These relationships are socially and physiologically beneficial but improve physiological responses as well.

Unlike those in Laub and Sampson's study, NOHSAP individuals did not get cut off from crime due to military careers, but due to other desistance factors. The institutions of marriage, religion and stable employment were more important to this population. Individuals who shared a routine, whether it be with a spouse, a church or an employer, were more likely to desist. These individuals found a meaningful social relationship and an accompanying structure that helped them find housing, get off of drugs and quit committing criminal acts.

Helping individuals find employment and creating jobs in the community are also important implications. Like those in the work of Uggen (2000), individuals with arrest histories who were helped in finding employment were much less likely to recidivate than those with no employment opportunities. Programmes that help homeless, substance abusers and criminal offenders find and maintain employment after release from shelters, treatment centres or prison would be valuable in the process of desistance.

Surprisingly, individuals in this study who maintained long-term sobriety attributed it to social networks that were not affiliated with 12-step meetings. The 12-step philosophy that emphasises taking care of substance abuse problems before all others may lead to significant difficulties in the homeless population (Bazemore & Cruise, 1993; Wright, Donley, & Rayburn, 2011). This sample of New Orleans homeless substance abusers had broader needs than simply sobering up, specifically stable employment and meaningful personal relationships. The individuals in this study reported problems in going to 12-step meetings and found social networks among other institutions such as church, family and employment to be far more helpful.

Also important in the desistance process was human agency, having the will to change one's life. Individuals talked about making the choice to stop using drugs and denied structural influences (such as residential change). They took credit for turning their lives around, and this is noted in previous desistance literature on cognitive transformation (Giordano, Cernkovich, & Rudolph, 2002).

Some policy implications from these results focus on the importance of choosing a good life partner, the reduction of alcohol and drug use among abusers, and emphasising stable employment. Additionally, emphasising changes in social networks, spending time with people who are sober, and perhaps moving away (literally) from drug using friends and family, helped individuals desist. Generating positive social support (friends who do not use drugs or alcohol, exercise and eat right) is a policy implication from previous studies that is confirmed from these findings.

Follow-ups with a small sample of the original clients some two decades later serve to amplify these conclusions in the limited but important sense that the clients whom we found to be the most 'successful' in the long term were precisely those who found 'jobs, families or housing circumstances' that continued inebriation and dissolution *would* imperil, that is, those for whom positive life changes did result in a 'significant improvement'. Lives improve when people have things to live for – an obvious conclusion, perhaps, but nonetheless, an important one.

References

Bazemore, G., & Cruise, P. L. (1993). Resident adaptations in an alcoholics anonymous-based residential program for the urban homeless. *Social Service Review, 67,* 599–616.

Biglan, A., Hood, D., Borzovsky, P., Ochs, L., Ary, D., & Black, C. (1997). Subject attrition in prevention research. *Substance Use and Misuse, 32,* 1673–1678.

Clarridge, B. R., Sheehy, L. L., & Hauser, T. S. (1978). Tracing members of a panel: A 17-year follow-up. In K. F. Schuessler (Ed.), *Sociological methodology* (pp. 185–203). San Francisco, CA: Jossey-Bass.

Eckland, B. K. (1968). Retrieving mobile cases in longitudinal surveys. *Public Opinion Quarterly, 32,* 51–64.

Giordano, P. C., Cernkovich, S. A., & Rudolph, J. L. (2002). Gender, crime, and desistance: Toward a theory of cognitive transformation. *American Journal of Sociology, 107,* 990–1064.

Lucas, R. E., & Dyrenforth, P. S. (2006). Does the existence of social relationships matter for subjective well-being? In K. D. Vohsand & E. J. Finkel (Eds.), *Self and relationships: Conceptualizing intrapersonal and interpersonal processes* (pp. 254–273). New York, NY: Guilford.

Maner, J. K., Gailliot, M. T., & Miller, S. L. (2009). The implicit cognition of relationship maintenance: Inattention to attractive alternatives. *Journal of Experimental Social Psychology, 45,* 174–179.

Rayburn, R. L., Pals, H., & Wright, J. D. (2012). Death, drugs, and disaster: Mortality among New Orleans' homeless. *The Journal of Long Term Home Health Care, 13,* 1–11.

Thornton, A., Freedman, D. S., & Camburn, D. (1982). Obtaining respondent cooperation in family panel studies. *Sociological Methods & Research, 11,* 33–51.

Uggen, C. (2000). Work as a turning point in the life course of criminals: A duration model of age, employment, and recidivism. *American Sociological Review, 65,* 529–546.

Waite, L., & Gallagher, M. (2001). *The case for marriage: Why married people are happier, healthier, and better off financially.* New York, NY: Random House.

Wright, J. D., & Devine, J. A. (1995). Housing dynamics of the homeless: Implications for a count. *American Journal of Orthopsychiatry, 65,* 320–329.

Wright, J. D., Donley, A. M., & Rayburn, R. L. (2011). The drunk, the addicted, and the just plain shiftless? In J. D. Wright & A. M. Donley (Eds.), *Poor and homeless in the sunshine state: Down and out in theme park nation* (pp. 171–192). New Brunswick, NJ: Transaction Publishers.

Appendix 1

Expenses	Cost ($)
Stamps	17
Envelopes	5
http://www.intelius.com/Membership	
1 year	243
Digital voice recorder	65
Telephone microphone recorder	20
New Orleans map	9
Literature (books)	25
Lodging	
August 2010	180
Flight	
August 2010	100
Rental car	
August 2010	70
Gas	
August 2010	40
Meals	
August 2010	108
Batteries (for recorder)	4
Airport parking	
August 2010	20

(Continued)

Appendix 1. Continued

Expenses	Cost ($)
Mileage (to airport)	
November 2010	44
Lodging	
November 2010	234
Flight	
November 2010	80
Rental car	
November 2010	160
Gas	
November 2010	70
Meals	
November 2010	144
Airport parking	
November 2010	24
Mileage (to airport)	
November 2010	44
Mailings	0
Total cost of project	1706

Alcohol and the family

Woody Caan

Royal Society for Public Health, London, UK

From a UK Government perspective, most current public health approaches to alcohol focus on the behaviour of individuals (e.g. the *Nudge* towards changed drinking: Marteau, T.M., Ogilvie, D., Roland, M., Suhrcke, M., & Kelly, M.P. (2011). Judging nudging: can nudging improve population health? *BMJ*, *342*, 263–265) and, increasingly, psychiatric approaches focus on adjusting microscopic circuits within the brain of individuals [Caan, W. (2012). Defining addiction, with more humanity. *Contemporary Social Science*, *7*. doi: 10.1080/21582041.2012.683577 (published first online 28 May)]. Although it has been apparent for a long time that a major area where alcohol causes harm is within the family and that involving family members in interventions (e.g. *Social Behaviour and Network Therapy*) is effective in reducing harm, most services for addiction neglect families as either assets or liabilities for treatment [Alcohol Concern. (2000). *Britains' ruin*? London: Alcohol Concern; Caan, W. (2000a). Working with families. In *Working with families – making it a reality* (p. 102). Birmingham: NHSE West Midlands; Copello, A., & Orford, J. (2002). Addiction and the family: Is it time for services to take notice of the evidence? *Addiction*, *97*, 1361–1363]. In the UK, over 6% of adults grew up in a family where at least one parent drank excessively [Alcohol Concern. (2000). *Britains' ruin*? London: Alcohol Concern] and since at least 8% of children live now in such homes it is not surprising that I found the extra training staff in Parenting Programmes requested most often was for problems with alcohol [Caan, W. (2010). Fair society, healthy lives. Timing is everything. *BMJ*, *340*, 495]. This year we face a turning point: *The Government's Alcohol Strategy* has a narrow emphasis on 'supporting individuals to change' [HM Government. (2012). *The government's alcohol strategy* (p. 21). London: Home Office]. This article promotes a more balanced alcohol policy, where understanding family ties and the history and quality of relationships are recognised as important – and valuable.

Pain, shame, blame

For some topics it is very painful even to acknowledge their existence, let alone to engage with helping them. I am indebted to Orford (2012) for drawing my attention to the shock and dismay that greeted the novel *The tenant of Wildfell Hall* in 1848, in which the wife and child flee from a dangerous husband (whose grim alcoholic decline appeared based on Anne Bronte's own brother). During our inner-city project on domestic violence (funded by the Neighbourhood Renewal Fund) with the aim of engaging families of all ethnicities through community centres, several women in *every* group *readily* opened up to our female outreach workers about the hurts they had received. When the workers had established some rapport with the groups, they would always ask about any role of alcohol in this common abuse (about this the women never spoke spontaneously). Across religions and cultures, and age of the woman abused, it was almost universal that their male assailant was drunk before they were assaulted, especially in those cases with frequent attacks that caused injuries. As the women shared their stories with each other, *in every centre* another story would emerge. Perhaps weeping and sobbing with shame, one woman would disclose that she got drunk after being assaulted to numb the physical and emotional pain. Then others would confirm this pattern of behaviour in their home, too. The outreach workers were both professionals with experience of domestic abuse but after a few months of asking the 'alcohol' question they became too distressed by the anguished histories elicited, to continue the project. During our rural project on domestic violence (funded by Cambridgeshire County Council) most of our informants were local professionals trying to help violent households, ranging from the community policewoman to the school nurse.

> The first evening I walked around the small estate with the most reported assaults, it seemed very ordinary, but had an unusual smell .... I looked in the gutters and they were full of broken glass from bottles of spirits, and the smell was simply alcohol. That project was only funded for six months but two local women were murdered, separately, by jealous former partners. Ever since then, when teaching about alcoholism, I try to impress on students the need to recognise Morbid Jealousy and its implacable danger. (Michael, Mirza, Mirza, Babu, & Vithayathil, 1995)

Most families affected by parental drinking never suffer such extreme harm. The consultant psychiatrist Jane Marshall has unsurpassed experience of alcohol dependence across many, different settings and she reminds us that these families 'make do' with various compromises and an 'emotional distance' (Marshall, 2002, p. 88). However, she also summarises two common consequences of having an alcoholic member in the family:

- 'Incessant alcohol-related arguments between parents, domestic violence and child abuse all cause emotional suffering which cannot easily be quantified. This suffering has lasting effects on personality development and the ability to form trusting relationships'.
- 'The effects on the family may be more indirect, taking the form of financial hardship (due to loss of job or spending income on alcohol), divorce, death of a parent, being taken into care. Children from "alcoholic" families are prone to anxiety and low self-esteem.' (Marshall, 2002, p. 88).

The good news: when two or more family members can work *together* in support of an agreed programme of treatment, recovery from dependence is much more likely (Caan, 2000a).

A simple, functional description of 'the family'

Before proceeding to detail the impact of alcohol on it, what do I mean by the family?

There are many more elegant descriptions than I can offer. For example, anthropologist and psychologist C.G. Jung gave many accounts of the family, typified by his 1941 archetype of the *Kore* (Jung, 1941) in which every mother contains her daughter in herself and every daughter her mother and every woman extends backwards into her mother and forwards into her daughter over the generations which brings a feeling of immortality .... Such models of the family emphasise continuity. Alternative models of the family emphasise stability. At the Conservative Party Conference in 1993, John Major promoted respect for something called Family Values in his *Back-to-Basics* speech. In E.O. Wilson's Socio-biology, inspired by colonies of ants (Wilson, 1975) family members with some common *genetic* heritage *co-operate* in many different roles, through natural selection over aeons. None of the descriptions above can describe the range of families seen in 1 day, in primary health-care services.

My test for a practical description became one that could include two diverse 'families' I observed: a large Sikh network around London and a small group of New Age Travellers that fitted into one van. There are both extended and nuclear 'families', both biological relatives and reconstituted families, both long-term residents in a single household and dispersed families separated for migrant labour or military service. What do all these families have in common?

Most readers have seen a building site. The simple functional analogy I use is *Scaffolding* in which all the pipes are connected, some intimately and some more remotely. If one pipe is removed (bereavement) or added (birth) all the members are affected as the loading shifts across all the couplers in this structure. When excessive loading or insecure coupling is present, the whole structure can collapse. Individual tubes may be reassembled into new scaffolds, but all the elements composing each scaffold are linked. Scaffolding functions in construction, and for good or ill, over time each family constructs its own legacy, for example, the family history or family business. However, in my model the building to which the scaffolding is attached is not 'the family', only those *living members* who interact .... this analogy may disappoint Daoists and Lacanians but for simplicity in this article I will not address the 'ghosts' of past generations nor the hopes of children 'as yet unborn'.

Is alcohol good for us?

For balance, it is important to recognise that alcohol can have both benefits and costs.

Alcohol can have positive roles within families, such as the ritual use of champagne by the Royal Family to launch new ships. In different cultures, many rites of passage involve drinking. After 40 years of living in England, I accept that *weddings* would probably disappear here, if diverse groups of adults had to be trapped for hours in one space with many strange, future in-laws – unless the anxiolytic action of alcohol damped down their social anxiety. When new Fellows of my old college passed round the port after dinner, they were being inducted into a tradition shared across centuries. When my Godchildren took their first Communion their *families* shared in a proud moment repeated across millennia. Over 90% of UK adults choose to drink alcohol sometimes, so I will not say more about positive aspects already familiar to readers.

During my professional career, the balance of benefits and risks from alcohol seems to have shifted, with harmful aspects of drinking becoming more widespread (Gilmore & Sheron, 2007). Just in terms of health, alcohol contributes to about 6.3% of all male deaths and 7.6% of disability in men worldwide and 'thus is one the largest avoidable risk factors' (Rehm et al., 2009). Around the world, traditional patterns of drinking (by culture, gender and age group) are changing with a major shift of marketing towards the developing countries (Burki, 2010). In the East of England, we were astonished to find how much vodka or rum many teenage schoolgirls now drank, and how much physical, educational and emotional harm they had already experienced by age 15–19 years (McMunn & Caan, 2007). The median alcohol intake was 10 units on each of two 'heavy' nights of the week (usually starting just after finishing school on a Friday night). Not every adolescent drank and not all the young drinkers got drunk, but regular drunkenness had become the *norm*.

The horizontal coupling: parents

The *WHO European Alcohol Charter* agreed by the European Union includes the principle that:

- 'All people have the right to a family, community and working life protected from accidents, violence and other negative consequences of alcohol consumption.' (Eurocare, 2000, p. 8)

Eurocare (2000, p. 66) also cite the important negative impact of harmful drinking in relation to childhood well-being, described in terms of the *United Nations convention on the rights of the child*. A study of social work across England and Wales warned that children living with parents who have alcohol problems 'can have disturbing experiences and can become carers at a young age' and the child caseload generated by alcohol 'is under-recognised and under-estimated' while in practice 'there is a loss of confidence about working with the family as a group and few opportunities to develop the necessary skills' (Kearney, Levin, & Rosen, 2000, pp. 1, 48, 49). During an 8-year period I worked with half a dozen Sure Start Children's Centres. From the first Centre where about 37% of the mothers with infants were lone parents still under 20 years old, it became clear that unrecorded, harmful drinking often made the parental role more difficult and in particular made the construction of a *stable* 'family' life more difficult (Caan, 2000b). One inspiring GP vocational trainee based next door to that Centre undertook to combine a regular assessment of alcohol use by adults with her routine family practice: this efficient model for family health is something we are still talking about in 2012, in the All Party Parliamentary Group on alcohol misuse. Based on new data from the SIPS (2012) research programme, primary care staff can now detect harmful drinking in adults efficiently with just five questions (known as the *FAST* screening items).

A key skill in working with parents who have developed long-term dependence on alcohol is summarised by Al-Anon (1992, p. 4): to promote 'mutual respect and trust'. The case vignettes on Sex in the Alcoholic Marriage (Al-Anon, 1992) provide food for thought for improved professional practice, here.

Alcohol-related harm is fairly common. Laslett, Ferris, Dietze, and Room (2012) surveyed parents or other carers in 1142 Australian families: 22% reported that the children had been affected by another's drinking in the last year with 3% reporting 'a lot' of harm. Education, income, gender and age of respondent had no association with prevalence of harm, but alcohol-related harm to children by another was reported by 41% of the single parents. That seems consistent with what we saw among vulnerable, lone parents in England, above, except we only saw a few single fathers in that sample. The setting where I met about 60 lonely young fathers, typically with a history of using both alcohol and drugs, was in prison (Caan, 1991). The good news: becoming better 'Dads' to their young children was the major motive for their seeking a life free of addictions after release from prison.

Parental substance misuse is a major risk factor for child maltreatment. It is estimated to be a factor in 80% of child maltreatment cases in the USA (Reading et al., 2009). Within child protection, maltreatment can affect more than one child in the family, and in the UK alcohol misuse is particularly associated with maltreatment of *all* children in the family (Gilbert et al., 2009). A Norwegian study of 8984 school children found that 'children of alcohol abusers enjoy being at school as much as other children' (Torvik, Rognmo, Ask, Roysamb, & Tambs, 2011, p. 3) but their attention and conduct in lessons was worse than other children, with those children who reported seeing their parents drunk having especially poor school adjustment. The World Mental Health Survey of 51,507 households in 22 countries found 4877 people with any substance use disorder (7.7% total) including 4443 with clinical 'Alcohol Abuse' and 1595 with chronic Alcohol Dependence (McLaughlin et al., 2012). Across *all* psychiatric diagnoses surveyed there was a significantly increased likelihood of *Offspring* developing a mental disorder if either Parent had a history of misusing substances (i.e. mainly alcohol). However, the greatest risk to children was them *also developing substance misuse*.

The odds ratios for this increased risk to offspring:

- just father misused = 2.0
- just mother misused = 2.2
- both parents misused = 3.6

Adoption studies suggest two main genetic patterns for boys developing alcoholism, one with adult onset and one with juvenile onset. The contribution of genes is most apparent in those family trees where both biological fathers and sons develop serious problems in adolescence, but even in those families, over 80% of sons never develop alcoholism (Caan, 2002). Environmental (nurturing) factors unconnected with their inheritance protect them from that biological risk.

The vertical coupling: children

Young people can also develop harmful drinking. When we evaluated a pathfinder Children's Trust (Chalmers, Gant, Brind, & Caan, 2006), referrals came from many sources and disruptive behaviour in school or anti-social behaviour during the holidays were the main reasons for referral. The peak age group for referral was between 10 and 12 years, i.e. around the transition from primary to secondary education. We expected to see lots of emotional difficulties related to their problem behaviours, but what surprised me was how the majority of these young boys and girls were getting drunk, habitually. In the words of one nearby Charity, these school children felt they were 'fireproof' when it came to substance use .... although they were alarmed by an increasing experience of self-harm, and a group of slightly older adolescents produced a play about alcohol and teenage pregnancy based on several recent cases in their school.

Alcohol has a characteristic effect on the mind in situations when there is a 'conflict' between the possibility of an action leading to *either* reward *or* punishment (Caan, 2002, pp. 52–53). Alcohol gives that *Dutch courage* where young drunks ignore the risks to just go for the pleasure. The 15-year-old Joy Rider I met who regularly drank half a bottle of vodka before driving around the dark streets at high speed (McKay & Caan, 2002) had no idea of the risks he was taking until one afternoon he sat down with our school nurse, sober, to review his life. Today more and more 15-year-old residents of the UK drink to get drunk (Caan, 2011) and my preliminary observations with the Victims and Vulnerable Young Persons initiative suggest that in the communities where such behaviour is widespread every Friday and Saturday night, the whole community pays a heavy price.

The issue is really one of good or bad trajectories of growth, across the totality of a young person's development. In the steering group for the strategy *No health without mental health*, we reached a complete consensus on these recommendations:

- 'prioritise early intervention across all ages;
- take a life course approach, with objectives to improve outcomes for people of all ages' (HM Government, 2011, p. 13).

It is easy but unhelpful to blame children: in his American polemic *Don't let your kids kill you*, Rubin (1996) bemoans under 'What price parenthood?':

- 'you're like a lot of parents who've been living out a horror film, with your drugged or drunken kids assuming the starring roles ...' (p. 4).

That 'horror' is unlikely to have appeared overnight or entirely to possess just *one* twisted pole in the system of family 'Scaffolding'. Problem drinking usually develops gradually (Caan, 2002) and by the time alcohol dependence is evident, it typically appears within a context of multiple difficulties (Caan, 2009) where professionals truly need 'the necessary skills' (Kearney, above) to prioritise the goals for intervention, with the individual – and all significant others.

Through many media, young people in the UK are bombarded with messages promoting underage drinking (Cassidy, 2012). In the All Party Parliamentary Group, we have discussed access to 'cheap booze' with a range of stakeholders, including advisers from Scotland where they are debating legislation on a minimum price per unit of alcohol. In the current English strategy, the spotlight on youth drinking is projected onto just the '120,000 most troubled families in the country' (HM Government, 2012, p. 22). Members with 'alcohol dependence' are a feature of these families of trouble-makers (HM Government, 2012, p. 22) but the focus on this population does not originate from health concerns, but is a consequence of last year's riots in England (Fletcher, Gardner, McKee, & Bonell, 2012) coupled with the economic concern of the Secretary of State for Work and Pensions that family breakdown is costing the Government £20 billion per year (Duncan Smith, 2012). Ireland sees similar problems with youth drinking but within the wider context:

- 'It is unrealistic to expect strategies aimed at the prevention of problem drinking by young people to succeed if these strategies are solely focused on young people and ignore the drinking habits of the adult population.' (Barnardos, 2002, p. 12).

School-based alcohol education needs to be integrated with wider public policy on alcohol (Barnardos, 2002). Initiatives in English schools do not have a good track record including my own marked failure around alcohol, within Personal Social and Health Education (Caan, 2009). Parenting initiatives such as the Strengthening Families Programme (cf. Caan, 2010) offer an opportunity to reach the parts of our population that other community groups cannot reach ... but will the new statutory Health and Wellbeing Boards plan for large numbers of families with previously unknown needs for help with alcohol? The Voluntary and Community sector could have a key role here, as demonstrated in the promising *family alcohol project* for London (Caan, 2001). In their International review, Jackson, Geddes, Haw, and Frank (2011) found long-term benefits from one intervention developed in a high-crime area that combined work with primary school teachers, schoolchildren and their families: the Seattle Social Development Project.

Adding more floors

The oldest and youngest generations are easily forgotten in alcohol policy.

Prospective studies of foetal alcohol effects are rare, although Leigh-Anne Davies recently presented her prospective work in South Africa to Alcohol Research UK and I hope this important research will be published soon. Retrospective lessons about pregnancy (Caan, 1996) suggest that there could be many opportunities to prevent alcohol-related disabilities in offspring, which currently affect roughly 1% of UK children .... but the current health inequalities for antenatal services mean that even if staff had the right training, the mothers who most need help are most likely to miss out. Abnormalities in facial growth can be detected at birth (the Foetal Alcohol Syndrome) but the most common effects of alcohol on early development only appear as children enter school with a *spectrum* of mild learning disabilities or persistent behaviour problems.

In terms of older people, the best predictor of disability in men at the age of 70 years is their past alcohol consumption at the age of 40 years (Vaillant & Mukamal, 2001). For both men and women, we know alcohol-related liver disease is on the increase in the UK, and reflecting similar histories of heavy drinking Gupta and Warner (2008) warn of a coming epidemic of alcohol-related dementia. We do not know how family carers will respond to the onset of such alcoholic dementia.

I am indebted to Moos, Schutte, Brennan, and Moos (2010) for caution around prejudging older drinkers. Heavy alcohol consumption in *surviving*, older couples who have achieved long-term stable marriages may not be associated with difficulties in family functioning!

The scaffold collapses

Looking back on the childhood adversity associated with their parents' alcohol problems, offspring report they were frequently worried about family instability (Velleman & Orford, 1990). In Russia, parental alcohol dependence is recorded in two-thirds of all cases of child maltreatment, mainly neglect leading to children being placed in residential care (Gilbert et al., 2009). Unfortunately such residential care is a high-risk environment for subsequent physical and sexual abuse. The charity Turning Point (2011) found that many of their alcohol-dependent clients had children, but 52% of these parents said they were unable to provide them with adequate care because of their drinking and many were separated from their children.

In England, the family drug and alcohol court is being piloted with the aim of preserving families where possible, even in the presence of additional problems such as insecure housing, debt or domestic violence (Rix, 2012). Family-friendly services for alcoholism are rare in the UK but one promising therapeutic approach is *Social behaviour and network therapy* (Copello & Orford, 2002). The social workers Forrester and Harwin (2011) reviewed 185 child-care cases in terms of good (47%), mixed (31%) and poor outcomes (22%: where more problems developed over time). Parental alcohol misuse was a feature of three-quarters of cases with poor outcomes, including most of those where children had suffered significant harm. However, in all 12 cases where parents 'significantly reduced or stopped' their drinking (Forrester & Harwin, 2011, p. 103), there were good outcomes. They offer this advice for such cases:

- 'Focus on the child not the drug or alcohol problem' (p. 138)

Parents who are in the caring professions are not immune to family problems. In our study of sick doctors, Stanton and Caan (2003) found many sought help for a combination of problems: alcohol dependence, depression and family breakdown.

Policy action

A global lesson from the WHO is to combat stigma and promote rights (Hock et al., 2012). During the First World War, pressure in America to prohibit alcohol sales was linked to women's right to vote and to protect the welfare of the family. But women also played a decisive role in repealing the Prohibition legislation later, to combat the threats to family life from both increased criminality and criminalisation (Rose, 1996). Today, I am very worried about the possible stigma in being labelled a 'troubled family' (above) although this policy might have the indirect effect of making many services think about developing more family-friendly provision. Other UK policies around advertising alcohol to young people or minimum pricing need to be impartially evaluated. A useful resource for this is the new *Public Health Outcomes Framework* that includes both direct measures of harm (such as alcohol-related admissions to hospital) and indirect indicators (such as domestic abuse, under-18 conceptions and mortality from liver disease: Department of Health, 2012).

Reflections and limitations

So far I have written from a very personal perspective. It is important to recognise that there is a rich history of research on alcohol and the family (Barnes & Augustino, 1987). There are significant dimensions that I have not been able to address here, including housing, employment and alcohol (Caan, 2001). Alfred Adler (1870–1937) had been a general practitioner and family practitioners will notice that I have not addressed the unconscious processes that shape the development of different personalities within one family or the degree of co-operation that develops within the framework represented by my crude Scaffolding analogy. Many of Adler's ideas of belonging and connectedness can best be illustrated today in the *Five ways to wellbeing* promoted by the new economics foundation (NHS Confederation, 2011).

Conclusion

The Government's Alcohol Strategy has a narrow emphasis on 'supporting individuals to change' (HM Government, 2012, p. 21). A deeper understanding of the origins and impact of dangerous drinking within a family context may help future Commissioners and Providers of services deliver more acceptable and effective interventions. In some families this may even change an intergenerational history of harm to a more hopeful legacy.

References

Al-Anon. (1992). *The dilemma of the alcoholic marriage.* New York, NY: Al-Anon Family Group Headquarters, Inc.

Alcohol Concern. (2000). *Britains' ruin* London: Alcohol Concern.

Barnardos. (2002). *Families under the influence* (Every Child Matters report). Dublin: The National Children's Resource Centre.

Barnes, G. M., & Augustino, D. K. (1987). *Alcohol and the family: A comprehensive bibliography.* Westport, CT: Greenwood Press.

Burki, T. (2010). Changing drinking patterns: A sobering thought. *Lancet, 376,* 153–154.

Caan, W. (1991). Preliminary observations on a drugs & AIDS initiative for prisoners in the South West Thames health region. *British Journal of Addiction, 86,* 1516.

Caan, W. (1996). Foetal alcohol related developmental deficit: A chance for mental health promotion in primary care? *The Network Developing Mental Health in Primary Care, 2,* 3.

Caan, W. (2000a). Working with families. *Working with families – making it a reality* (p. 102). Birmingham: NHSE West Midlands.

Caan, W. (2000b). Sure start in practice. *Up Start! 2,* 4.

Caan, W. (2001). Coming together on alcohol and drugs: A capital idea. *Journal of Mental Health, 10,* 477–479.

Caan, W. (2002). Alcohol on the mind. In W. Caan & J. de Belleroche (Eds.), *Drink, drugs and dependence: From science to clinical practice* (pp. 51–68). London: Routledge.

Caan, W. (2009). Misfortunes never come singly. *Perspectives in Public Health, 129*(5), 210–211.

Caan, W. (2010). Fair society, healthy lives. Timing is everything. *BMJ, 340,* 495.

Caan, W. (2011). How family friendly is the UK? *BMJ, 343,* 331–332.

Caan, W. (2012). Defining addiction, with more humanity. *Contemporary Social Science, 7.* doi: 10.1080/21582041.2012.683577 (published first online 28 May).

Cassidy, S. (2012, May 17). Alcohol adverts 'target teenagers' despite strict code. *The Independent,* 11.

Chalmers, S., Gant, M., Brind, L., & Caan, W. (2006). *Children's trust evaluation report.* Chelmsford: Essex County Council.

Copello, A., & Orford, J. (2002). Addiction and the family: Is it time for services to take notice of the evidence? *Addiction, 97,* 1361–1363.

Department of Health. (2012). *Healthy lives, healthy people: Improving outcomes and supporting transparency.* London: DH.

Duncan Smith, I. (2012). *Social justice: Transforming lives, strategy launch.* Retrieved from http://www.dwp.gov.uk/newsroom/ministers-speeches/2012/13-03-12.shtml

Eurocare. (2000). *Alcohol problems in the family. A report to the European Union* (2nd ed.). St. Ives: Eurocare.

Fletcher, A., Gardner, F., McKee, M., & Bonell, C. (2012). The British government's troubled families programme. A flawed response to riots and youth offending. *BMJ, 344,* e3402 (published first online 16 May).

Forrester, D., & Harwin, J. (2011). *Parents who misuse drugs and alcohol: Effective interventions in social work and child protection.* Chichester: Wiley-Blackwell.

Gilbert, R., Widom, C. S., Browne, K., Fergusson, D., Webb, E., & Janson, S. (2009). Burden and consequences of child maltreatment in high-income countries. *Lancet, 373,* 68–81.

Gilmore, I., & Sheron, N. (2007). Reducing the harms of alcohol in the UK. *BMJ, 335,* 1271–1272.

Gupta, S., & Warner, J. (2008). Alcohol-related dementia: A 21st-century silent epidemic? *British Journal of Psychiatry, 193,* 351–353.

HM Government. (2011). *No health without mental health.* London: Department of Health.

HM Government. (2012). *The government's alcohol strategy.* London: Home Office.

Hock, R. S., Or, F., Kolappa, K., Burkey, M. D., Surkan, P. J., & Eaton, W. W. (2012). A new resolution for global mental health. *Lancet, 379,* 1367–1368.

Jackson, C., Geddes, R., Haw, S., & Frank, J. (2011). Interventions to prevent substance use and risky sexual behaviour in young people: A systematic review. *Addiction, 107,* 733–747.

Jung, C. G. (1941). The *psychological aspects of the Kore.* In (J. Chodorow, Trans., 1997) *Jung on active imagination* (pp. 154–157). Princeton, NJ: Princeton University Press.

Kearney, P., Levin, E., & Rosen, G. (2000). *Alcohol, drug and mental health problems: Working with families.* London: National Institute for Social Work.

Laslett, A-M., Ferris, J., Dietze, P., & Room, R. (2012). Social demography of alcohol-related harm to children in Australia. *Addiction, 107,* 1082–1089.

Marshall, E. J. (2002). Alcohol and society. In W. Caan & J. de Belleroche (Eds.), *Drink, drugs and dependence: From science to clinical practice* (pp. 82–92). London: Routledge.

Marteau, T. M., Ogilvie, D., Roland, M., Suhrcke, M., & Kelly, M. P. (2011). Judging nudging: Can nudging improve population health? *BMJ, 342,* 263–265.

McKay, I., & Caan, W. (2002). Free expression: Tailoring health services to young offenders in Barking & Dagenham and Havering. *Listen to me: Consulting young people on health and health issues* (pp. 91–100). London: Barnardo's, Right Fit series.

McLaughlin, K. A., Gadermann, A. M., Hwang, I., Sampson, N. A., Al-Hamzawi, A., Andrade, L. H., … Kessler, R. C. (2012). Parent psychopathology and offspring mental disorders: Results from the WHO World Mental Health Surveys. *British Journal of Psychiatry, 200,* 290–299.

McMunn, V., & Caan, W. (2007). Chlamydia infection, alcohol and sexual behaviour in women. *British Journal of Midwifery, 15,* 221–224.

Michael, A., Mirza, S., Mirza, K. A. H., Babu, V. S., & Vithayathil, E. (1995). Morbid jealousy in alcoholism. *British Journal of Psychiatry, 167,* 668–672.

Moos, R. H., Schutte, K. K., Brennan, P. L., & Moos, B. S. (2010). Personal, family and social functioning among older couples concordant and discordant for high-risk alcohol consumption. *Addiction, 106,* 324–334.

NHS Confederation and New Economics Foundation. (2011). *Five ways to wellbeing. New applications, new ways of thinking.* London: nef.

Orford, J. (2012). *Addiction dilemmas. Family experiences from literature and research and their lessons for practice.* Chichester: Wiley-Blackwell.

Reading, R., Bissell, B., Goldhagen, J., Harwin, J., Masson, J., Moynihan, S., … Webb, E. (2009). Promotion of children's rights and prevention of child maltreatment. *Lancet, 373,* 332–343.

Rehm, J., Mathers, C., Popova, S., Thavorncharoensap, M., Teerawatananon, Y., & Patra, J. (2009). Global burden of disease and injury and economic cost attributable to alcohol use and alcohol use disorders. *Lancet, 373,* 2223–2233.

Rix, J. (2012, February 1). A families man. *The Guardian,* (London), p. 35.

Rose, K. D. (1996). *American women and the repeal of prohibition.* New York, NY: NYU Press.

Rubin, C. (1996). *Don't let your kids kill you. A guide for parents of drug and alcohol addicted children.* Rockport, MA: Element Books.

SIPS. (2012). *Alcohol screening and brief intervention in primary health care*. PHC Factsheet. London: Institute of Psychaitry.

Stanton, J., & Caan, W. (2003). How many doctors are sick? *BMJ*, *326,* s97–s98.

Torvik, F. A., Rognmo, K., Ask, H., Roysamb, E., & Tambs, K. (2011). Parental alcohol use and adolescent school adjustment in the general population: Results from the HUNTS study. *BMC Public Health*, *11,* 706. Retrieved from http://www.biomedcentral.com/1471-2458/11/706

Turning Point. (2011). *Bottling it up: The next generation*. London: Turning Point.

Vaillant, G. E., & Mukamal, K. (2001). Successful aging. *American Journal of Psychiatry*, *158,* 839–847.

Velleman, R., & Orford, J. (1990). Young adult offspring of parents with drinking problems: Recollections of parents' drinking and its immediate effects. *British Journal of Clinical Psychology*, *29,* 297–317.

Wilson, E. O. (1975). *Sociobiology: The new synthesis*. Cambridge, MA: Harvard University Press.

The borders of booze Britain: alcohol controls and nationality

Tom Henri

Department of Social, Therapeutic and Community Studies, Goldsmiths, University of London, New Cross, London, UK

This article seeks to understand how UK alcohol control policies, historically and currently, are both informed by and seek to inform how we conceptualise the nation and nationality. Using the latest minimum price per unit of alcohol policy as a point of departure and setting it the context of over 300 years of alcohol controls, this article exposes how the internal contradictions inherent in alcohol regulation are obscured by the deployment of nationalism as a rhetorical device.

Introduction

This article argues that, both historically and in the current era, policies regarding the control of the sale and use of alcohol have as much to do with notions of nationality and the nation state as they do with public health, economy or crime and disorder.

The current UK coalition government has recently announced a policy of minimum price per unit for alcohol sales (Leicester & O'Connell, 2012). Although there is a chance that the European Union could overturn this policy under anti-competition laws, the policy raises many interesting questions of class and nationality as they relate to drinking. By setting a minimum price, this policy could be viewed as akin to a regressive taxation on drinkers, a sin tax to use John Stuart Mill's parlance (Mill, 1859), although clearly this is not a tax in the normative fiscal sense as no extra duties will be collected by the treasury. By setting the minimum price per unit of alcohol, prices of expensive, therefore exclusive, beverages will be unaffected, yet the cost of the cheapest supermarket and off-licence sold alcoholic drinks will increase. Therefore, we can say without much doubt that the consumers of cheap drinks, and therefore most likely the poor, are to be greatest affected by minimum price setting. As the price is set per unit of alcohol contained in the drink and not by the overall volume of the beverage, the greatest increase in cost to the consumer will be those who consume cheap yet strong drinks. As others have observed, there is an element of class conceit to this policy (Brockley, 2012) as the stated aim is to reduce binge drinking, the thinking behind the policy must therefore assume that binge drinking is a malaise of the poor, that the better-off do not engage in such behaviour, or if they do, there are no negative social or public health consequences of this behaviour. Thus, it is relatively straightforward to argue that there is a class dimension to this policy; while this is clearly important for a number of reasons, this article will argue that there is also an issue of nationality that is embedded in this policy, as there has been in many attempts to control the sale and consumption of alcohol throughout the modern history of Britain. The conjecture of this article is that this latest attempt to manage alcohol use can be utilised to reinforce notions of nationality and consequently has the potential to be used as leverage to reinforce national border controls.

This article will first provide a distilled history of alcohol control policies in the UK to illustrate how alcohol has been used historically to reinforce divisions of nationality and to construct the other. As Holt (2006) observes;

> Alcohol is a very useful lens through which to explore larger and more obvious historical changes such as industrialisation and the rise of the state. (p. 1)

Both processes (industrialisation and the rise of nation states) have, instrumentally or as a consequence, created social divisions and had enduring implications for notions of culture and identity. With industrialisation, there have been profound effects on the class structure along the lines of the ownership of the means of production and the division of labour (Marx, 1976). Others have argued that post-industrialisation also has an impact on class and alcohol consumption (Haywood & Hobbs, 2007), with the growth of the nighttime economy as a political and economic response to a post-Fordist paradigm. However, as stated, the focus of this article is not the relationship between alcohol consumption and social class; however, it is worth keeping in mind the how notions of social class, and certainly social class deficit, inform debates and policies about the consumption of alcohol beverages. Rather, the focus of this article is to explore how alcohol controls relate to discourses of nationality.

As recent as 2004 the then British Prime Minister Tony Blair gave a speech referring to binge drinking as the 'new British disease' (Rayner, 2004), as we will uncover; how and how much the British drink has often been used to construct a sense of national pride and deficit both for those identified as British and those identified as non-British. From the Irish who 'revels in drink to the point of the most bestial drunkenness' (Engels, 1993, p. 103) of nineteenth century Manchester to the late twentieth century demonisation of 'lager louts' (Mares, 2001, p. 153), alcohol has been used as a marker of nationality and national identity. Therefore, we will explore how the current policy paradigm of minimum alcohol unit price fixing continues this tradition by looking at in whose interest this policy benefits. At this stage of the analysis, we will see that both the alcohol industry and the criminal fraternity are set to profit from the policy. Given the commonly perceived ideological standpoint of the current UK coalition government, it may be obvious as to why they might wish to support the corporate brewing industry, it is well known that the alcohol industry is a great supporter of the incumbent Conservative Party (Bower & Cox, 2010), what is initially less obvious is to why the government would want to support organised crime, as a clear consequence of minimum price setting is likely to be an increase in both the volume of alcohol smuggling and in the profits to be made from such nefarious activities. As we will see, this policy gift to those engaged in unlawful business could provide the subtext for further policy shifts in relation to nationality and nationhood. Finally this article will look at how the implementation of the alcohol minimum price setting policy could be utilised to provide the justification for enhanced border controls. If increasing the price of legally available alcohol does lead to an increase in contraband, then there may be calls to tighten UK border controls, thus, in the final analysis, this article is interested in the relationship between 'booze Britain' and 'Fortress Britain'.

As this article will explore, alcohol has for centuries defined who we are in terms of nationality, as by extension, defined who is the other or outsider. If this is framed as an issue of nationality, then it must also be an issue of borders. For without borders, even if they may be elastic and porous, it is challenging to either define the nation or any sense of imagined community which may be corollary to the construction of nationality (Anderson, 1991). Historically, attempts to control the sale and consumption of alcohol have had some effect on how the nation-state practices border controls (Ludington, 2006). This article is focused on the context of the UK, but we could also use the impact of the 18th amendment to the US constitution as a comparative example. The prohibition of alcohol led to a massive growth in illegal bootlegging, or alcohol smuggling. This in turn, provided the US Coastguard Service with further policing roles in order to stem the supply of illegal alcohol being imported into the USA.

A distilled historical context

In order to provide the historical context to the proposition of this article, will involve the analysis of some key events of three historical epochs; The Act of Union with Scotland and London's Gin Craze of the eighteenth century; Irish immigration and industrialisation in the nineteenth century and binge drinking and the accession of eight Eastern European countries to the European Union at the beginning of the twenty-first century. As we will see, the relationship between how we consume alcohol and how we conceptualise nationality is not new. This section on the history of alcohol consumption in Western contexts is not exhaustive but rather provides exemplars that according to Holt (2006):

> [...] not even the commercial interests that control the production of alcohol can totally regulate, much less control, either the meaning or myriad functions of alcohol in Western life. (p. 7)

The first era considered in this article, the early to mid-eighteenth century, has two artefacts that have a bearing on the relationship between alcohol control and the nationality. Edinburgh is the epicentre for one series of events whereas London sets the scene for another set of independent events, however both narratives evoke notions of national identity, and both also have a bearing on relations with the French.

Starting in Scotland, Ludington (2006) examines how French claret wine became the preferred drink of the Scots around the time of the Act of Union. Before the Act of Union, claret was popular in Scotland whereas it was not so in England, this could be due to differences in taxation and duty regimes. However, the Act of Union and equalisation of duties dramatically raised the cost of imported claret in Scotland, for English duties on French wine were more costly. Instead of having the effect of reducing claret consumption in Scotland, the increase in duty, according to Ludington's research, only served to increase the illegal importation of claret. At least part of the evidence for the popularity of claret in Scotland before the Act of Union was the Wine Act of 1703, which according to Ludington (2006), 'established claret as a symbol of Scottish independence and as a commodity to symbolically defy the English' (p. 167). England was at war with France and therefore the drinking of French wine could be viewed as an act of defiance. Furthermore, the English duties on imported alcohol, which were relevantly steep as compared with those of the pre-Union Scots, were in part to pay for the war against France. Thus, the act of drinking French claret had a two-fold influence on the Scots relationship with the English; first as a symbol of defiance and second by being financially able to enjoy more luxurious wine. Thus, through this period, we can observe how the consumption of a certain alcoholic beverage, namely claret, was used to both define and reinforce Scottish nationality as superior to that of the imperialistic English. As the Scot William Clelland wrote from London in 1705,

> All the wine here is poison'd and all the women pox't at least I would fain fancie so whylst I have no monie. (Ludington, 2006, p. 169)

However, if we take Ludington's treatise beyond the Act of Union of 1707, which lead to the equalisation of alcohol duties on French wine between Scotland and England, we see that claret consumption in Scotland did not necessarily reduce, rather it propagated, the illegal importation of claret as a further act of defiance. This increase in claret smuggling, therefore served two purposes: it increased the profit from importation of wine, as no duty was being paid, and it reinforced the popular opposition to the new customs and duties (Ludington, 2006, p. 172)

At the same time as the Scottish were imbibing claret as a symbol of opposition to English imperialism, London was experiencing a alcohol consumption frenzy popularly referred to as the 'gin craze', as exemplified by Hogarth's 1751 print 'Gin Lane' with its depiction of morally deficient behaviour brought on by the overconsumption of gin. Much has been written about the impact and the attempts to control Londoners' taste for gin in the eighteenth century; however, in thinking about nationality we need to look at the causes of the gin epidemic.

Gin was first popularised amongst the English at the beginning of the eighteenth century by soldiers returning from the continent after involvement in the war of Spanish succession (Maples, 2012). At that time, the most popular alcoholic beverage in England was beer. However, the distillation and production of gin was vigorously promoted by the English government. The perceived rationale for this was two-fold: first to boost the rural economy by creating a new market for grain producers and second, to create a domestic challenge to foreign imports, particularly French brandy (Holt, 2006). The French at this point were in hostilities with the English. In order to achieve these aims, the importation of spirits from foreign countries was duly banned and no licence was required for the production of gin, unlike alehouses (Maples, 2012). Therefore, gin was cheap and plentiful with few obvious competitors. These conditions lead to the extreme consumption of gin by the poor of London, seemingly a cheap and available distraction from the harsh conditions of living in London at that time. At the height of the 'gin craze' Londoners were consuming over 11 million gallons of gin a year (Maples, 2012). It is worth bearing in mind that at this time London's population was between one and one and a half million, which gives some idea of the vast quantity of gin the populace of the capital were consuming. The social impact of this gin epidemic is well documented (Maples, 2012), including increased mortality, crime, disorder and child mortality. Yet given the unprecedented detriment to health and social well-being, it took the British authorities nearly 50 years to get on top of the problem after a succession of botched legislation (Maples, 2012).

So, the gin craze of the eighteenth century had its roots in both economic policy and through the process of defining and reinforcing the nation-state. As the Scots were consuming claret to define and reinforce their sense of national identity also Londoners were doing as a response to a series of policies to promote the English economy and English independence in a hostile European context. Thus, by looking at the historical context of the eighteenth century, we see that some of the themes that underscore our contemporary concerns regarding 'booze Britain' and Blair's new British disease of binge drinking have some echoes down the ages.

If we look at some features of nineteenth century England, we can identify further themes that have some contemporary resonance. As we saw before, it was an Act of Union with Scotland in the eighteenth century that had an effect on popular practices and rituals around alcohol. Thus, the Act of Union of 1801 with Ireland must also have some bearing on how we came to view the Irish, as a problematic drinker in the context of industrial England. Taking Engels famous description of the Irish in Manchester in the middle of the nineteenth century as a point of departure

> And since the poor devil must have one enjoyment, and society has shut him out of all others, he betakes himself to the drinking of spirits. Drink is the only thing which makes the Irishman's life worth having, drink and his cheery care-free temperament; so he revels in drink to the point of the most bestial drunkenness. The southern facile character of the Irishman, his crudity, which places him but little above the savage, his contempt for all humane enjoyments, in which his very crudeness makes him incapable of sharing, his filth and poverty, all favour drunkenness. The temptation is great, he cannot resist it, and so when he has money he gets rid of it down his throat. What else should he do?

> How can society blame him when it places him in a position in which he almost of necessity becomes a drunkard; when it leaves him to himself, to his savagery? (Engels, 1993, pp. 103–104)

Engels classic ethnography describes the Irish immigrants of Manchester in less than favourable terms. However, it must be noted that Engel's thesis was to document the alienation of Manchester's working class during the industrial revolution. Although Engel's identifies the Irish as almost savage in nature and divisive to working class solidarity by providing a wage drag, or even through the importation of scab labour, we could interpret Engel's description as symptomatic of the lumpenproletariat, Marx's reserve army of labour (Marx, 1976). Indeed, a close reading of the Engels passage alludes to some sympathy for the plight of the Irish worker,

> How can society blame him when it places him in a position in which he almost of necessity becomes a drunkard; when it leaves him to himself, to his savagery? (Engels, 1993, p. 104)

However, we choose to read this passage, it is self-evident that Engel's identifies the Irish with drunkenness. However, citing *The Report on the State of the Irish Poor in Great Britain*, E.P. Thompson contextualises the drinking behaviour of the Irish in manufacturing England:

> On the Saturday night, when they receive their wages, they first pay the score at the shop ... and their rent ... and when their debts are paid, they go drinking spirits as long as the remnant of their wages holds out. On the Monday morning they are penniless. (Thompson, 1963, p. 476)

So, depending on one's reading of Engels and Thompson, it can be implied that excessive drinking with which the Irish poor appear to be associated with, can be viewed as either a moral deficit of nationality or as a solace from exploitation, poverty, discrimination and dislocation.

As both authors observe, the plight of the Irish working poor in England in the nineteenth century is an amalgam of the effects of war, famine, unskilled work, low wages and Diaspora. Nevertheless, as Thompson (1963) notes, '[...] Irish labour was essential for the Industrial Revolution [...]' (p. 473) as their labour was cheap, relative to English workers, and they were demoralised to the point that they would undertake the 'most disagreeable kind of course labour' (Thompson, 1963).

Consequently, constructing the Irish immigrant of industrial England as having the character of 'most bestial drunkenness' (Engels, 1993, p. 103) enabled the further exploitation by the industrial bourgeoisie in the accumulation of capital and the suppression of workers' wages. So our evidence of the relationship between notions of nationality and the consumption of alcohol continues to have resonance from the eighteenth century and into the nineteenth century.

If we take this conception of the impoverished, hardworking and drunk Irish immigrant forward over one hundred years to the beginning of the twenty-first century and replace 'Irish' with 'East European', the similarity of popular discourse in the UK is startling. While we could frame the popular notion of the bestially drunk Irish migrant as part of the lumpenproletariat of the Industrial Revolution, we can view the popular image of heavy drinking East European migrants as part of the precariat of our current epoch (Standing, 2011).

The accession of the eight east European countries (Cyrus, Czech Republic, Estonia, Hungary, Latvia, Lithuania, Malta, Poland, Slovakia and Slovenia – collectively known as the A8 countries) to the European Union in 2004 resulted in the UK Government putting into place:

> [...] transitional measures to regulate A8 nationals' access the labour market (via the Worker Registration Scheme) and to restrict access to benefits. (Mills, Knight, & Green, 2007, p. 4)

However, as Standing notes, when it comes to economic immigration, governments often claim, '[...] they are limiting migration while facilitating the growth of a low-wage disposable labour supply.' (Standing, 2011, p. 91). Whereas the Irish in nineteenth century England provided the 'course labour' (Thompson, 1963, p. 476) for the Industrial Revolution, A8 immigration provides a similar role in advanced capitalism of the reserve army of labour by responding to the needs of flexibilised labour markets, becoming part of a high risk, low wage, insecure labouring class Standing refers to as the precariat (Standing, 2011).

As stated in the introduction to this article, social class is an important aspect of alcohol policy but for the purposes of this argument we need to put this to one side, as nationality is our focus. This is not to deny that that there are important, valid and relevant intersections between class and nationality, however let us not confound the argument.

Discussion

So our brief journey through some key eras of British history reveals that at times the Scottish, the English, the Irish and the Polish (for the Polish are the largest nationality to move to the UK following the A8 accession (Mills et al., 2007)) have all been, and to varying degrees still are, defined and identified in terms of their approach to the drinking of alcoholic beverages. Many of these often played out in stereotypes of popular culture. The question remains, how did problematic, excessive, heavy or binge drinking become an issue so seemingly entwined with Britishness? From 'booze Britain' to Blair's new British disease to Brits abroad, the popular notion seems to be of the behaviour of the British is rather unpleasantly alcohol-fuelled. Furthermore, what ideological function does this notion the excessively imbibing Brit perform? For it must be ideological as the evidence suggests that despite the hype and the hyperbole, British alcohol consumption has been falling for several years (Morgan, 2011). Furthermore, the apparatus of alcohol regulation, as Valverde (1998) observes, '[...] does not seek to maximize health but rather to organize and regulate consumption, producing ordered, disciplined drinkers' (p. 144). She goes on to state:

> Liquor licensing and control systems, whatever their particularities, all share the difficult position of having the regulation of personal consumption as their objective – an objective rather out of keeping with the logic of liberalism. (Valverde, 1998, p. 145)

This gives us a useful lens to develop conjecture to understanding the rhetoric of 'British' problem drinking. Utilising the ideologies of the nation and nationality as a framework for advocating controls and regulation of alcohol consumption, policy-makers, and those who seek to influence them, can neatly sidestep this internal contradiction. Foregrounding a perceived national problem of disordered drinking and therefore rallying behind the flag of the health of the nation allow governments to enforce regulation without appearing at odds with the underlying political ideology of deregulation and laissez-faire policies. Furthermore, by acknowledging the post-Fordist nighttime economy agenda of contemporary post-industrial Britain, one could deduce that using the proxies of both public health and law and order to regulate alcohol consumption enables the continued development and investment in an economically-potent alcohol industry while appearing to pour scorn on its social consequences. By deploying the evocative ideology of nationality, which as Anderson notes is so powerful as a rhetorical device that citizens will wilfully die for its cause (Anderson, 1991), governments can scaffold policies for the regulation of individual behaviour while seemingly appear not at odds with the underlying political doctrine of deregulation and reification of markets. This prioritising of the needs of the market, as Adorno opines, leads to the dominance of the exchange-value of commodities, this dominance obscures the original use-value allowing the commodity to take on a new use-value that can be any number of cultural associations and assumptions (Adorno, 1991). Alcohol is one such commodity whereby the new use-value contains cultural associations and assumptions we could package as nationality or nationalism.

The new policy agenda

The current UK government's recent policy announcement regarding alcohol minimum price setting seemingly has two groups of clear beneficiaries and one group of losers. The losers are those who buy cheap alcoholic beverages, as the policy will increase the cost of drinking regressively to the poorest. The potential winners from this policy are primarily the alcoholic beverage industry and secondly those involved in the illegal importation of alcohol. According to the Institute for Fiscal Studies, fixing the price per unit at 40p (which is the government's proposal) would lead to transfers of revenues of up to £850 million per year to the alcohol industry (Leicester & O'Connell, 2012), although this figure does not account for any behaviour changes as a result of the policy, it clearly demonstrates the potential benefit to the alcohol industry. Also, as this policy does not constitute a duty, there will be no increase in revenue to the treasury. Potentially the opposite is true, if the policy has its stated desired effect of reducing alcohol consumption, then the treasury is going to lose income from alcohol duties. This policy seems to lack coherence in terms of political philosophy, as British Prime Minister David Cameron stated, 'This is a national problem and it needs a government to focus on it', words that would have John Stuart Mill inebriated with fury, yet this is a government which has set about the retrenchment of social policy like none before. As Valverde (1998) observes, all attempts at alcohol control have a poor logical 'fit' with liberalism. Licensing laws, controls on sales and consumption, and prohibition all create impediments to free markets, yet states that enact extreme forms of controls, for example, some Islamic states, to not experience a crisis of legitimacy. This then raises the question of how the state, any state not just theocracies, can have systems that control alcohol at all. Raising the spectre of the nation-state and applying it to notions of national deficiency enables the State to differentiate alcohol as distinct from other forms of beverage in special need of control and management. Evoking the mantra of 'booze Britain' as a national deficiency enables the furthering of controls on the sale of alcohol, seemingly without contradiction, in the context of (neo-) liberalism.

Increasing the price of low-cost alcoholic beverages in the UK could have a significant impact on the frequency and profitability of alcohol smuggling. According to the figures from HM Revenues and Customs (UK Government agency tasked with both collecting duties and enforcing borders), the alcohol smuggling industry costs the exchequer £1.2 billion per year in unpaid duties (Norman, 2012) and that much of the business of alcohol trafficking is controlled by 'organised criminals' (HMSO, 2010). As with the Scottish consumption of claret with the equalisation of duties and tariffs after the Act of Union had an effect on the quantity and profitability of illegal alcohol smuggling in the eighteenth century, it would be foolhardy to believe that increasing the minimum price per unit of alcohol will not have an effect on the illegal alcohol trade. This thought exposes another internal contradiction of the minimum alcohol price policy. On one hand the policy evokes the idea of nationality as a vehicle to deploy regulation of individuals within the nation, yet on the other hand, it provides the incentive for increasing criminal activities at the borders of the nation. As previously stated, nationalism requires a nation and the nation requires boundaries, although these boundaries may be both elastic and porous, therefore it is the boundaries of the nation in some way define nationality. Consequently, there is a significant poverty of logic with the policy itself. For it would appear contradictory to deploy the nation as a rhetorical device while seemingly setting the scene for increasing the strain on the national borders which increased illegal smuggling will inevitably create. Yet maintaining or indeed strengthening national borders is one area of policy that the current UK government seems keen to develop. However, border control is an area of public policy which in itself is fraught with contradictions. Politicians of many persuasions wish to be seen to highly manage and regulate border controls to counterbalance popular fears regarding immigration and its perceived strain on social provision, housing stock and employment opportunities, yet to over-control borders would have profound effects on the economic well-being of the country, as global capital flows require, to some degree, the freedom of movement of peoples and commodities. Thus, for those invested with making border control policy, this requires a balancing act using a range of policy and rhetorical devices to retool the balance from time-to-time. The conjecture of this article is that the alcohol minimum price per unit of alcohol policy has the potential to be deployed, in the future, as one of these devices. If we consider hypothetically that at some point in the future there is a perceived need to reinforce border controls, for example, an increase in people entering the UK to seek asylum, then evidence of increased alcohol smuggling could provide the basis for the securing of border controls. Thus fears about loss of revenue, increasing crime and continued access to cheap alcohol beverages could be used as a precursor to shoring up the border of fortress Britain. In the masquerade of border control policy, any increase in smuggling as a result of the minimum alcohol pricing policy is a useful disguise with which to protect the nation.

Last orders (conclusions)

As we have seen, how we use alcohol and how the state attempts to regulate the use of alcohol has long been tied to notions of nationality and nationalism. The current policy agenda of minimum price per unit fixing continues this tradition. It is somewhat ironic that the policy is likely to be challenged by the European Union, because as we have seen Britain's relationship with other European nations has often been the catalyst for alcohol control policies.

The argument that the state's dealings with alcohol have had a long association with understanding the nation and nationality is compelling, however the potential to use this policy as a precursor to strengthening or reinforcing national borders is somewhat worrying as it suggests a degree of premeditated deceit. This argument is purely conjecture, but there seem few other reasons for the UK coalition government to pursue a policy which has significant advantages for organised criminals.

From the historical analysis, it is striking how pervasive alcohol has been, and continues to be, as a lens to view nationality, particularly as a deficit. From the gin craze of eighteenth century London, via the bestially drunk Irish of the nineteenth century to the street drinking Accession Eight nations of the twenty-first century, alcohol has continued to provide a prism to view the shortcomings of national characteristics.

Furthermore, alcohol control policies have a long history of both influencing and being influenced by how national borders are understood and operated. From eighteenth century duties on imported French brandy to the development of the powers and responsibilities of the US Coastguard Service during the period of national prohibition, we can cite several examples of attempts to control the importation of alcoholic drinks have lead to the development of smuggling to either avoid law enforcement or customs and duties.

It would be easy to reduce these challenges and contradictions of alcohol controls to an economic imperative. The UK alcohol industry is powerful, both economically and politically, but commercial interest, in and of itself, cannot account for cultural understandings of alcohol as they relate to nationality and borders, neither can a class analysis, although there are class dimensions to both popular ideas about alcohol consumption and policies to control its consumption. The evidence from eighteenth century Scotland demonstrates this well. The fact that the Scots continued to imbibe claret after the Act of Union has little to do with commercial imperative and not much to do with class antagonisms. Rather it was symbolic of Scottish independence and defiance of the English. Again, if we consider London's eighteenth century gin craze, commercial interest and class analysis do not tell the whole story. Although there was an economic interest in promoting gin as a popular beverage, and its effects were, on the whole, felt by the poor, it was as much to do with England's relationship, or rather lack of relationship, with the French that gave rise to the chronic use of gin in eighteenth century London. If we look forward from the eighteenth century, through the nineteenth century into our current time, how we understand the nation and nationality continues to inform our understand of alcohol and its control.

The popular notion of booze Britain continues this tradition of conflating commercial interests, notions of class deficit and nationality. This is somewhat symptomatic of the internal contradictions of alcohol control policies. These policies are supposed to objectively regulate consumption but this does not fit well in the context of the current dominant political ideology. By foregrounding issues of nationality, policy-makers can at the very least attempt to obscure this profound contradiction. It is this reification of the nation state and nationality that enables the differentiation of alcohol from other consumable commodities as distinct and in need of control.

Another contradiction involves the impact of the alcohol minimum pricing policy on the government of the British nation. If the impact of the policy is that the consumption of legally available alcohol reduces and the consumption of illegally imported alcohol increases, then this will inevitably result in reduced revenues for the UK treasury. Furthermore, the potentially increased strain on controlling the national border could create further expenditure for the UK government.

To conclude, this latest policy agenda, of minimum price setting per unit of alcohol, could be viewed as a response to a popular discourse on the state of the nation commonly referred to as 'booze Britain'. This notion of national deficit has been employed as a rhetorical device in order to impose regulation on the drinkers of Britain. This policy, in turn, has significant potential consequences for how the British state operates its border controls. Any changes to the operation of national borders have consequences for conceptualising the nation and therefore the notion of nationality. So, the debate comes round full circle, a policy which has been informed by a popular discourse of nationality has the potential to then either shift or reinforce the notion of the nation and nationality.

References

Adorno, T. W. (1991). *The culture industry: Selected essays on mass culture*. London: Routledge.

Anderson, B. (1991). *Imagined communities*. London: Verso.

Bower, J., & Cox, H. (2010). *Political influence and hostile bids: How Scottish & Newcastle became the UK's largest brewer*. Paper presented at the 14th Annual Conference of the European Business History Association, University of Glasgow, Glasgow.

Brockley, B. (2012). Drunkenness is a right not a privilege. Retrieved from http://brockley.blogspot.co.uk/2012/02/drunkenness-is-right-not-privilege.html

Engels, F. (1993). *The condition of the working class in England*. Oxford: Oxford University Press.

Haywood, K., & Hobbs, D. (2007). Beyond the binge in 'booze Britain': Market-led liminalization and the spectacle of binge drinking. *The British Journal of Sociology*, *58*(3), 437–456.

HMSO. (2010). *Renewal of the 'Tackling Alcohol Fraud' strategy*. Retrieved from http://customs.hmrc.gov.uk/channelsPortalWebApp/channelsPortalWebApp.portal?_nfpb=true&_pageLabel=pageExcise_ShowContent&id=HMCE_PROD1_030554&propertyType=document

Holt, M. (2006). *Alcohol: A social and cultural history.* Oxford: Berg.
Leicester, A., & O'Connell, M. (2012). *How significant is a minimum unit price for alcohol of 40p*? London: Institute for Fiscal Studies.
Ludington, C. (2006). 'To the king o'er the water' Scotland and Claret, c. 1660–1763. In M. Holt (Ed.), *Alcohol: A social and cultural history* (pp. 163–184). Oxford: Berg.
Maples, T. (2012). Gin and Georgian London. In History Today (Ed.), *Last orders: A social history of drinking* [Kindle edition] (Chapter 4). London: History Today.
Mares, D. (2001). Gangstas or lager louts? Working class street gangs in Manchester. In M. Klein, H. Kerner, C. Maxson, & E. Weitekamp (Eds.), *The Eurogang paradox: Street gangs and youth groups in the US and Europe* (pp. 153–164). London: Kluwer Academic.
Marx, K. (1976). *Capital* (Vol. 1). London: Penguin.
Mill, J. S. (1859). *On liberty.* London: Longman, Roberts and Green.
Mills, K., Knight, T., & Green, R. (2007). *Beyond Boundaries: Offering substance misuse services to new migrants in London.* London: Centre for Community Research, University of Hertfordshire.
Morgan, J. (2011). Why is alcohol consumption falling? Retrieved April 24, 2012, from http://www.bbc.co.uk/news/magazine-12397254
Norman, J. (2012). *Illegal alcohol and tobacco sales.* London: Hansard. Retrieved from http://www.publications.parliament.uk/pa/cm/cmtoday/cmwhall/01.htm
Rayner, J. (2004). On the streets of binge Britain. Retrieved March 27, 2012, from http://www.guardian.co.uk/travel/2004/sep/05/restaurants
Standing, G. (2011). *The precariat: The new dangerous class.* London: Bloomsbury.
Thompson, E. P. (1963). *The making of the English working class.* London: Penguin.
Valverde, M. (1998). *Diseases of the will: Alcohol and the dilemmas of freedom.* Cambridge: Cambridge University Press.

Minimum pricing for alcohol: a Millian perspective

Ben Saunders

Philosophy, University of Stirling, Stirling, UK

The Scottish National Party (SNP) has recently sought to introduce minimum pricing for alcohol in order to tackle drink-related problems. This paper outlines what the prominent nineteenth-century liberal reformer John Stuart Mill would have said about such a proposal. Mill's 1859 *On Liberty* argued that the only legitimate reason for the state or society to interfere in an individual's conduct is to prevent harm to others, rejecting paternalistic interventions or moralistic legislation. After outlining Mill's general position, this paper gathers a number of his scattered remarks on alcohol. It seems that he would be prepared to endorse a number of restrictions on the sale of alcohol, including age restrictions, mandatory health warnings and even anti-social behaviour orders for those guilty of violent crime when drunk. Nonetheless, Mill is clear that the state has no right to prohibit alcohol and, for the same reasons, that the state has no right to increase its cost for purpose of deterring drinking – a measure that, Mill argues, differs only in degree from outright prohibition. Thus, according to Mill, the proposal of the SNP oversteps the bounds of legitimate government interference, unjustly interfering in individual liberty. Interestingly, however, Mill allows that governments have the right to tax inessential goods for purposes of raising revenue, which suggests that the government could legitimately tax alcohol, provided its reasoning was not (as the SNP has stressed its is) to deter people from drinking.

The Alcohol etc. (Scotland) Act 2010, which came into force in October 2011, bans price promotions that make it cheaper to purchase alcohol in larger quantities (such as 3-for-2 deals) and thereby possibly encourage people to drink more than they otherwise would have done. As I write, the Scottish government is proposing further measures to curb drinking, to include a minimum price per unit of alcohol (The Scottish Government, n.d.). This is not its first attempt to introduce minimum pricing. The Scottish National Party (SNP) proposed a minimum price, then set at 45 pence/unit, in the previous parliament, when operating as a minority government (British Broadcasting Corporation, 2011). With the SNP now being a majority in Holyrood (the Scottish parliament), the chances that a new bill will be successful are much increased. Moreover, the issue of alcohol pricing is not by any means a peculiarly Scottish one. As I was putting the finishing touches to this paper, news broke that the Westminster government is considering a similar measure in England and Wales (British Broadcasting Corporation, 2012). This makes the matter of alcohol pricing one for urgent attention.

A full assessment of this pricing policy is, of course, beyond the scope of a single paper. It would depend, in particular, on further theoretical and empirical investigation into its likely consequences. For purposes of the present paper, I shall grant to proponents of minimum pricing that the consequences of this measure would be as they predict.[1] My question is whether these consequences would legitimate such a measure. I shall not, however, provide a definitive answer, even to this question. Rather, my aim is merely to set out what the influential nineteenth-century liberal John Stuart Mill would have said about minimum pricing.

Mill's ideas, as expounded in his 1859 essay *On Liberty*, have exerted significant influence on public policy. It is often noted that the 1957 Wolfenden Report (or Report of the Departmental Committee on Homosexual Offences and Prostitution), which recommended the decriminalisation of homosexuality in the UK, employed essentially Millian reasons (e.g. Moffat, 2005, pp. 1098–1099; Tebbit, 2000, pp. 113–117). Other commentators have discussed how Millian principles might be applied to the regulation of various activities, including pornography (Dyzenhaus, 1992; Vernon, 1996), genetically modified food (Holtug, 2001), hate speech (Brown, 2008), quarantine law (Parmet, 2008) and reproductive cloning (Burley, 2008; Moffat, 1998, pp. 587–595). Some of these commentaries focus on interpreting Mill's own views, while others are more speculative extrapolations of his views to other areas, but all assume that we can learn something important from seeing what Mill, or a contemporary Millian, might say about the issue in question. Mill is taken to be an exemplar of the liberal tradition or at least one prominent strand within that tradition, and *On Liberty* thus serves to show how such liberals might reconcile the value of individual liberty and need for social regulation. We may not agree with Mill's conclusions on any given issue, and I do not attempt to *defend* them here, but they represent one particularly influential way of approaching problems of social regulation. Thus, when debating public policy on some given matter, it is worth considering what Mill might say about it, in order to have a clear statement of the liberal position. We might, ultimately, choose to reject this, favouring, for instance, a more conservative stance, but if we do, then the onus is on us to answer Mill's arguments.

My aim here is to outline a Millian approach towards alcohol and, in particular, to the Scottish government's minimum pricing proposal. Since alcohol is a matter that Mill explicitly touches upon at several points in *On Liberty*, my goal will be to provide a faithful reconstruction – rather than speculative extrapolation – of his views. I shall begin by outlining Mill's general thesis, before considering its implications for alcohol policy. Only after examining a Millian approach to alcohol as a whole do I turn to what he might have said about the Scottish government's minimum pricing policy. I conclude that Mill would probably have considered this policy unjustified, because its stated intention is paternalistic, but – perhaps ironically – he would have allowed the government to tax alcohol, with much the same effect.

1. The harm principle

Mill's (1977) *On Liberty* famously defended the view that

> the sole end for which mankind are warranted, individually or collectively, in interfering with the liberty of action of any of their number, is self-protection ... [i.e.] to prevent harm to others. His own good, either physical or moral, is not a sufficient warrant. (p. 223)

This so-called harm principle has had a profound impact upon public policy, but its interpretation has been the subject of much controversy among commentators. It is frequently complained, for instance, that Mill does not provide any account of what constitutes harm, thereby leaving the application of this principle indeterminate.

In fact, Mill does have an account of harm that rests upon his utilitarian moral theory. As he goes on to say,

> I regard utility as the ultimate appeal on all ethical questions; but it must be utility in the largest sense, grounded on the permanent interests of man as a progressive being. Those interests, I contend, authorize the subjection of individual spontaneity to external control, only in respect to those actions of each, which concern the interest of other people. (Mill, 1977, p. 224)

The account that Mill offers of happiness in his *Utilitarianism* is also the source of much controversy (Brink, 1992; Saunders, 2010, 2011; Sturgeon, 2010). For present purposes, one important element of Mill's view is that though individuals ought in almost all cases to be left free to live as they choose, this is *not* because individuals are *infallible* judges of their own good. Sometimes, individuals may wrongly think that something is good for them when it is not. Conversely, sometimes they may wrongly think that something harms their interests when it does not. If Mill is concerned only with true or objective harms, then not everything that we take to be harmful is in fact grounds for interference. Waldron (1987) employs such a line to argue that 'moral distress', or offence at having one's deeply held convictions challenged, is not a harm, because it is not something that we have a genuine interest in avoiding.

Setting aside, for the moment, the question of when interference in individual liberty *is* justified, Mill states that it is *not* justified to interfere with someone's conduct for his or her own good, either physical or moral. This is generally taken to represent a prohibition on two kinds of interference, namely paternalism and legal moralism. Put briefly, paternalism is interfering with another's conduct for her own good, whether that be to make her life go better or to prevent her from harming herself (Arneson, 1980). Legal moralism is the view that it is the business of the law to uphold moral standards as such and thus that the law may prohibit, for example, homosexuality or the eating of pork (Mill, 1977, p. 284) on the grounds that it is immoral. Mill (1977) suggests that these considerations are not reasons that justify interference with another's freedom:

> These are good reasons for remonstrating with him, or reasoning with him, or persuading him, or entreating him, but not for compelling him, or visiting him with any evil in case he do otherwise . . . . The only part of the conduct of any one, for which he is amenable to society, is that which concerns others. In the part which merely concerns himself, his independence is, of right, absolute. (p. 224)

Such remarks have led a number of interpreters to conclude that Mill's harm principle rests upon a distinction between 'self-regarding' and 'other-regarding' actions (Riley, 1991, pp. 15–16; Wollheim, 1973, p. 2). It is not permitted for society to interfere with an individual's actions, provided that they affect only himself, but it is permitted to interfere if his actions also affect others. This distinction is, however, problematic (Rees, 1991, pp. 172–174; Wollheim, 1973, pp. 26–27). Moreover, I have argued elsewhere that it does not fit Mill's intentions (Saunders, n.d.). Suppose, for the sake of argument, that we could distinguish self-regarding and other-regarding actions. Some acts might indeed be purely self-regarding, and therefore immune to interference, for instance, masturbating within the privacy of one's own house. But many acts that we do affect others, at least indirectly.

To be sure, Mill is not committed to saying that the fact that someone is harmed by my conduct is sufficient reason to interfere. Harm to others is necessary, but not sufficient, to justify intervention (Rees, 1991, p. 185; Riley, 1991, p. 16). Nonetheless, if we think that all other-regarding conduct can *in principle* be interfered with, then you might seek to prevent me from marrying the person of my choosing on the grounds that the person is not good enough for me. That is, if Mill's harm principle is reduced to the view that we cannot intervene in self-regarding conduct, but may intervene in other-regarding conduct, then you might justifiably intervene *paternalistically* (i.e. for my own good) in my conduct, provided that it also affects others. This, I assume, is not Mill's intention.

I propose that the harm principle is better interpreted *not* as a distinction between *actions* that can permissibly be interfered with and actions that cannot, but rather as that between justified *reasons* for interference and reasons that are not adequate grounds for interference. While this interpretation is by no means unanimously accepted, it is endorsed by a number of others (e.g. Mulgan, 2011, p. 118; Rawls, 2007, pp. 290–292; Skorupski, 1989, p. 343; Ten, 1980, pp. 40–41). Recall that Mill speaks of whether certain *ends* warrant interference. Moreover, his objection to paternalism is an objection to certain reasons for intervention. Whether my restriction of your liberty is paternalistic or not depends upon my reasons for it. It is only paternalistic if consideration of your good is at least one of my reasons for interference, but I might interfere solely for some other reasons (say, to prevent you from harming me) in a way that merely happens to serve your interests too and this would not be paternalistic. Thus, one and the same intervention might or might not be consistent with Mill's harm principle, depending upon its justification.

Consider a ban on homosexuality. One putative justification runs as follows: (i) fulfilling relationships are an important part of leading a good life, (ii) homosexual relationships cannot be fulfilling, therefore (iii) homosexual relationships are an impediment to leading a good life. While this argument may rest upon a false premise, and hence provide no justification whatsoever, my point is that the justification that it *purports* to give is paternalistic: people should be prevented from entering homosexual relationships because such relationships prevent them from having truly fulfilling heterosexual relationships. An alternative justification for prohibiting homosexuality, however, is that it is morally wrong, regardless of any effect it has upon practising homosexuals. Again, we might question whether it is indeed wrong or whether it is the law's business to prohibit all moral wrongs, but the point is that this putative justification is moralistic. But now suppose that a ban on homosexuality is proposed in order to combat the spread of sexually transmitted diseases (STDs), such as AIDS. Once again, we may think that this is not an adequate justification for the measure it is supposed to justify, but it is entirely consistent with Mill's harm principle: the purpose of this restriction is to prevent harm to others, rather than to promote the good of those interfered with or to enforce the community's accepted moral standards.

I propose that we take Mill's harm principle as a restriction upon the *reasons* that can justify interfering in someone's liberty. The only reasons that can justify such intervention are those that appeal to harm to others. Thus, paternalistic reasons carry no justificatory weight, even if the action to be interfered with does affect other people. It follows that self-regarding actions are in general immune to interference, because the only possible reason there might be to interfere cannot apply, since self-regarding actions (by definition) cannot harm others.[2] Based on this view, we cannot tell whether an intervention is justified simply from knowing what is to be interfered with; we need to know the reasons for interference. Of course, people may have multiple intentions behind a single action. I may interfere with your conduct in order to both protect others and protect you. But in this case, Mill's position is that the paternalistic reasons carry no weight: my intervention is justified only if the harm thereby prevented *to others* would be enough to justify interfering with your liberty. Moreover, where possible, we should seek ways to prevent this harm without limiting your freedom (if this is possible and less costly, then limiting your freedom is not justified, since it is not necessary in order to prevent the harm).

One worry that someone might have with this approach is that someone may misrepresent his or her reasons. Suppose, for instance, that a religious conservative disapproves of homosexuality on moral grounds, but proposes prohibition for the ostensible purposes of combating the spread of STDs. It might look as if people's paternalistic or moralistic preferences are given free reign, provided that they can operate under cover of some harm-to-others-based reason. In fact, this is not so. Remember, based on the view proposed, paternalistic or moralistic reasons carry no weight when it comes to justifying policy. Thus, even if someone's *motive* for proposing intervention is his or her own paternalistic or moralistic inclinations, such intervention is only actually justified if there are sufficient harm-to-others-based reasons for intervention, independent of these other reasons. Mill (1985) is explicit that our motivation for acting need not be the same as what justifies our action, for instance, someone who saves another from drowning acts rightly even if he or she did so in hope of reward (pp. 219–220). If some action causes sufficient harm to others to justify banning it, then it does not matter whether one's motive for proposing a ban is, in fact, paternalistic: the ban is nonetheless justified.

2. Mill on alcohol

Having laid out the general contours of Mill's position, I now show how he would approach the regulation of alcohol, drawing, in particular, upon several passages in which he explicitly discusses either alcohol specifically or stimulants more generally. I shall postpone discussion of minimum pricing until the following section. Here, my aim is to establish the general way in which Mill applies his principle to the case of alcohol.

The first point to note is that which confines his defence of individual liberty to 'human beings in the maturity of their faculties' (Mill, 1977, p. 224). Children can permissibly be protected from themselves, as well as from others. Indeed, Mill (1977) comments that society has 'absolute power' over children during the early part of their existence (p. 282). His point, however, is that society has ample opportunity to instil in them the capacities to choose wisely. If, upon reaching adulthood, a person still desires to act in a manner that society deems bad, then the blame should fall on the society for failing to provide a proper education. Once people have reached adulthood, they have the right to decide for themselves how they wish to live, provided that they do not harm others. If they choose badly, then any harm that they suffer is their own responsibility and, moreover, will serve as a salutary example to others (Mill, 1977, p. 283). Thus, banning the sale of alcohol to minors is justifiable, but society has no right to regulate what adults do, except where necessary to prevent harm to others.

To be sure, Mill is not endorsing a life of idle drunkenness; his point is merely that if this is someone's choice and she does not harm others, then society has no business in trying to prevent her from wasting her own life. The harm that she suffers is enough, without society adding further punishment (Mill, 1977, pp. 279–280). To think otherwise, Mill (1977) argues, amounts to saying that

> it is the absolute social right of every individual, that every other individual shall act in every respect exactly as he ought; that whosoever fails thereof in the smallest particular, violates my social right, and entitles me to demand from the legislature the removal of the grievance. (p. 288)

This is a view that Mill (1977) rejects because

> it acknowledges no right to any freedom whatever, except perhaps to that of holding opinions in secret ... [and] ascribes to all mankind a vested interest in each other's moral, intellectual, and even physical perfection, to be defined by each claimant according to his own standard. (p. 288)

Not only does this leave little, if any, room for individual freedom, but it may simply be *impossible* to act in a way that offends no one. Suppose the Christians think it a violation of their social right if anyone does not worship the Christian God and no one but the Christian God, while the Muslims consider it a violation of their social right if anyone either does not worship Allah or worships anyone other than Allah. Whatever one does, in this society, will violate the self-defined social right of at least one of these groups.

Thus, Mill rejects the supposition that we have any right that others live as we would like them to. All we can insist upon is that their conduct not be such as to cause us harm. Simply being drunk is not, in itself, harmful to others and thus not something that society has the right to regulate. Society can only rightfully intervene if someone violates a specific duty to the public or causes perceptible hurt to others (Mill, 1977, p. 282).

> If, for example, a man, through intemperance or extravagance, becomes unable to pay his debts, or, having undertaken the moral responsibility of a family, becomes from the same cause incapable of supporting or educating them, he is deservedly reprobated, and might be justly punished; but it is for the breach of duty to his family or creditors, not for the extravagance. (Mill, 1977, p. 281)

Similarly, we may punish a policeman for being drunk *on duty*, but not simply for being drunk (Mill, 1977, p. 282). Presumably such considerations would also justify laws against, for example, drink-driving. But the mere fact that I find others' drunkenness distasteful, even disgusting, is no more grounds for interference than the fact that I dislike others' religious or sexual practices. I may seek to avoid association with these people, thereby exercising my own freedom (Mill, 1977, p. 278), or I might try to persuade them to change their ways (Mill, 1977, p. 277), but I have no grounds for coercing them.

Of course, this is all based upon the supposition that drinking alcohol causes no harm to others, but this might be disputed. We know, for instance, that some people are violent when drunk, as evidenced by the fights that break out on many city streets around pub closing time. Perhaps, it might be suggested, this gives us justifiable grounds for interfering, since here the reason is to prevent harm to others. It is true that, interpreted in the way that I have proposed (as a restriction upon reasons for interference, rather than on what actions can be interfered with), Mill's harm principle does allow us to interfere with conduct that is in itself harmless if this is necessary to prevent harms from occurring. We might, for instance, prohibit all cases of trespass, even if some are harmless, because doing so is the only way to prevent the harms that usually occur as a result (cf. Ripstein, 2006). Perhaps, then, we might be justified in restricting the consumption of alcohol, in order to prevent the harms that occur as a result of drunken violence.

This measure might be potentially *justifiable*, but it does not follow that it is actually *justified*. Preventing harm to others is a legitimate reason for intervention, but to know whether intervention is, all things considered, justified, we must balance the benefits (prevented harm to others) against the costs of intervention, including the loss of liberty for those restricted. Intervention is only actually justified if it does more good than harm. These considerations raise issues of proportionality. If harm can be prevented, while only prohibiting a narrow range of actions, then the prohibition may be justified, but if harm could be prevented only by prohibiting very many otherwise legitimate actions, then we may be better advised to tolerate the harm for the sake of freedom. Consequently, justified restrictions will in general restrict as little as possible, consistent with achieving their end.

We see one application of this reasoning in the fact that only drink-*driving* is restricted by law. Drink-drivers impose the risk of harm upon others as a result of their unsafe driving. Society may legitimately seek to prevent this risk. One way to do this is by criminalising driving after consuming alcohol. We might alternatively seek to prevent this risk (drink-driving) by banning consumption of alcohol entirely. This might be more effective in preventing the harm, but it would also involve a greater loss of liberty, since non-drivers would be deprived of the right of a harmless drink. The latter alternative is therefore unjustified, since the interference in liberty is greater than what is necessary in order to prevent the harm. Prohibiting drink-driving specifically is (almost) as effective at preventing the harm, but much less costly to liberty generally, and so more likely to be justified.

Mill himself offers a similar example concerning violent drunks. A general prohibition on alcohol might be the most effective way of preventing drunken violence, but it would again come at the cost of preventing responsible consumption of alcohol. Better, then, is to find some way of targeting only the violent drunks, as we target only drink-drivers. This is precisely what Mill (1977) suggests:

> Drunkenness, for example, in ordinary cases, is not a fit subject for legislative interference; but I should deem it perfectly legitimate that a person, who had once been convicted of any act of violence to others under the influence of drink, should be placed under a special legal restriction, personal to himself; that if he were afterwards found drunk, he should be liable to a penalty, and that if when in that state he committed another offence, the punishment to which he would be liable for that other offence should be increased in severity. The making himself drunk, in a person whom drunkenness excites to do harm to others, is a crime against others. (p. 295)

Mill proposes here something like anti-social behaviour orders (ASBOs), which target only those with a history of drunken violence. There is no need to prevent others from enjoying alcohol responsibly in order to punish violent drunks. To the extent that the SNP seeks to tackle drinking as a 'public order' issue, there are ways of doing this other than increasing the price of alcohol across the board, for instance, through ASBOs, curfews or laws against drinking in the streets. It would not be necessary to ban alcohol in order to preserve public order.[3] Consequently, measures targeting all alcohol consumption indiscriminately are illegitimate, whether paternalistic in intent or not, since they unnecessarily restrict people's liberty.

Mill's just-quoted remarks come in the context of his discussion of trade. Though, in general, Mill subscribes to laissez-faire principles of free trade, he also allows that there is a need for social regulation of trade. This is particularly the case when it comes to potentially dangerous goods, such as poisons. Once again, Mill (1977) thinks a blanket prohibition on all poisons unjustified:

> If poisons were never bought or used for any purpose except the commission of murder, it would be right to prohibit their manufacture and sale. They may, however, be wanted not only for innocent but for useful purposes, and restrictions cannot be imposed in the one case without operating in the other. (p. 294)

Nonetheless, for the purpose of restricting crime, it would be permissible to require all sellers of poisons to keep record of their sales. 'Such regulations would in general be no material impediment to obtaining the article, but a very considerable one to making an improper use of it without detection' (Mill, 1977, p. 295). In other words, the minor inconvenience of having one's transaction recorded is no loss of liberty to someone who wants the poison for legitimate ends and not, therefore, objectionable. Similarly, all poisons should be required to carry warnings, in order to prevent accidents, and this too is no violation of the buyer's liberty (Mill, 1977, p. 294).

What Mill says about poisonous substances seems to apply *mutatis mutandis* to alcohol. The government may legitimately require manufacturers to state the number of alcoholic units in a given drink, so that people know how much they are drinking. It might even require alcoholic drinks to carry health warnings, as cigarette packets do. These measures do not prevent those who wish to drink from doing so; they merely serve to warn them of the potential consequences of their actions, thereby ensuring that they freely accept any harms that might befall them as a consequence. In other words, while this might be paternalistic, it does not restrict anyone's liberty.

Furthermore, it is permissible for the state to regulate who may sell both poisons and alcohol and to impose certain conditions on the sale, provided that they are not too onerous on those who use these substances in permissible ways. Mill (1977) notes that

> All places of public resort require the restraint of a police, and places of this kind particularly, because offences against society are especially apt to originate there. It is, therefore, fit to confine the power of selling these commodities (at least for consumption on the spot) to persons of known or vouched-for respectability of conduct; to make such regulations respecting hours of opening and closing as may be requisite for public surveillance, and to withdraw the licence if breaches of the peace repeatedly take place through the connivance or incapacity of the keeper of the house. (p. 298)

Once again, it is permissible for the state to regulate the sale of alcohol, in order to reduce the risk of harm, provided that it can do so without appreciably restricting the freedom of others. Restrictions on when and where alcohol may be sold are permissible, provided that they not be too burdensome on people's liberty. For instance, it may be sensible to prohibit the sale of alcohol at petrol stations or to restrict it around football matches, in order to reduce the risk of drink-driving or crowd violence, but to allow only one licensed pub in any town or city would be too restrictive.

The state might also regulate the advertising of alcohol (and any other goods it deems fit). Mill (1977) allows that, in general, it should be permitted to advise or encourage others to do what it is permitted for them to do (p. 296). But against this general presumption, he also sees some merit in the alternative view that the state

> cannot be acting wrongly in endeavouring to exclude the influence of solicitations which are not disinterested, of instigators who cannot possibly be impartial – who have a direct personal interest on one side, and that side the one which the State believes to be wrong, and who confessedly promote it for personal objects only. There can surely, it may be urged, be nothing lost, no sacrifice of good, by so ordering matters that persons shall make their own election, either wisely or foolishly, on their own prompting, as free as possible from the arts of persons who stimulate their inclinations for interested purposes of their own. (Mill, 1977, p. 297)

If people freely choose to drink, then their choice must be respected, but it does not follow that the state should stand by and allow the producers or sellers of alcohol actively to encourage this through advertising.

Mill in general opposes state regulation of speech. He is adamant, for example, that the falsity of an opinion is not grounds to censor its expression (cf. Mill, 1977, pp. 243–252). Nonetheless, the context of expression matters. Mill's (1977) example is that it is permissible to express the view that corn-dealers are starvers of the poor through the press, but not to incite an angry mob outside a corn-dealer's house (p. 260). Similarly, we might restrict slogans such as 'Guinness is good for you.' We might hold that it should be allowed within, say, a scientific study on the health effects of alcoholic beverages, but not in any form of advertising. The state does not restrict *what* is said, but, as with licensing, it may restrict *when* or *where* things can be said.

Since the concern with advertising arises out of a concern about solicitation or inducement, the same reasons might also apply to promotional offers. We may, that is, worry if people are being induced to drink more than they otherwise would because the sellers and manufacturers of alcohol make it more attractive, for instance, through special offers or incentives. For instance, if pubs or supermarkets are allowed to run 'buy one, get one free' offers, then someone who only wanted one drink might well end up having two. It seems that Mill was alive to such concerns and his remarks upon solicitation suggest that whether or not he would have allowed such practices, he certainly did not regard them as unproblematic. The Scottish government's existing legislation, prohibiting certain special offers on alcohol, is not therefore *obviously* contrary to Mill's harm principle. This, however, turns us to the issue of alcohol pricing.

3. Alcohol pricing

Thus far, we have seen that though Mill seeks to protect a sphere of individual spontaneity and freedom from social intervention, his harm principle allows him to impose considerable restrictions upon alcohol, including controls on when and where it may be sold and who to and on advertising. But if the state may regulate the sale of alcohol, we might think that the state could *de facto* ban it, by greatly restricting the circumstances in which it was sold. Such measures would not, of course, prevent people from brewing and drinking their own alcohol, but they would greatly reduce the consumption of alcohol. Mill (1977) was aware, however, that restricting the sale of a given commodity, such as alcohol, also serves to restrict its use:

> Selling fermented liquors, however, is trading, and trading is a social act. But the infringement complained of is not on the liberty of the seller, but on that of the buyer and consumer; since the State might just as well forbid him to drink wine, as purposely make it impossible for him to obtain it. (p. 288)

Since it is not permissible for the state to prohibit the consumption of alcohol, it is also not permitted for it to use its otherwise legitimate powers of regulation in order to prevent (entirely or merely to some degree) such consumption. As we have seen, Mill allows that the state may legitimately regulate when and where alcohol can be sold, but this is to prevent harm to others, rather than to prevent the consumption of alcohol as such. One and the same restriction can be legitimate if implemented for one purpose, but illegitimate if implemented for some other purpose, as shown by the earlier example of homosexuality. Thus, while the state may have legitimate reasons to restrict the sale of alcohol, discouraging drinking is not one of them:

> The limitation in number, for instance, of beer and spirit houses, for the express purpose of rendering them more difficult of access, and diminishing the occasions of temptation, not only exposes all to an inconvenience because there are some by whom the facility would be abused, but is suited only to a state of society in which the labouring classes are avowedly treated as children or savages, and placed under an education of restraint. (Mill, 1977, pp. 298–299)

The state may have good reasons to restrict the number of public houses, but stopping adults from drinking as it sees fit is not one of them and amounts to unjustified paternalism (if for the good of those individuals).

Mill makes similar remarks concerning alcohol pricing. It is not legitimate for the state to increase the price of alcohol for the purpose of discouraging people from drinking:

> To tax stimulants for the sole purpose of making them more difficult to be obtained, is a measure differing only in degree from their entire prohibition; and would be justifiable only if that were justifiable. Every increase of cost is a prohibition, to those whose means do not come up to the augmented price; and to those who do, it is a penalty laid on them for gratifying a particular taste. (Mill, 1977, p. 298)

We might question whether merely increasing the price of something (here alcohol) is really analogous to prohibiting it altogether. Remember, however, that Mill allows that they differ in *degree*; his claim is that this difference in degree does not amount to a difference in *kind*. Suppose the government introduced a minimum price of £1000 per unit of alcohol. This would effectively prohibit all, bar the very rich, from purchasing alcohol (and thus from consuming it, unless either stolen or home-brewed). If we grant that this is an effective prohibition, however, then it seems that we must concede that a minimum price of 45p per unit is different only in degree and, likewise, an effective prohibition for those who cannot afford this. It might be responded that there is some point between 45p and £1000 at which the difference in degree becomes a difference in kind, but it is not obvious where that point would be (perhaps it differs for each potential consumer), and we might always ask whether there really is any significant difference between two prices either side of this point.

Mill's claim is that if paternalistic reasons cannot justify prohibiting alcohol, then they cannot justify making it more expensive either, for this is of a kind with prohibition. An increase in the price of alcohol, Mill might say, is equivalent in practice to fining those who drink it.[4] Paternalistic reasons, recall, may be 'good reasons for remonstrating with him, or persuading him, or entreating him, but not for compelling him, or visiting him with any evil in case he do otherwise' (Mill, 1977, p. 224). Thus, Mill recognises that others may interfere with our liberty in ways that stop short of compulsion. To prevent someone from drinking is a restriction of his or her liberty, but so is threatening him or her with punishment if he or she drinks. Some contemporary philosophers have denied this. Steiner (1994), for instance, holds that one is only unfree to do something if one is unable to do it, so threats or punishment do not diminish one's liberty (pp. 22–32). Perhaps Mill could concede that there is a sense in which one remains free to drink, even if threatened with punishment for doing so, so long as this threat still requires justification and cannot be legitimated by paternalistic reasons, any more than physical prevention.

Whether or not we accept Mill's argument, it seems likely that he would reject the Scottish government's minimum pricing policy. The only legitimate reason for the state to interfere in an individual's conduct is to prevent harm to others. While attempts to curb drinking may have this aim, it would not require a general prohibition on drinking, but rather should be targeted at those instances of drinking that impose the risk of harm on others, such as drink-driving or drinking for those with a history of drunken violence. There is no need for the state to impede the freedom of those who drink responsibly, either by banning alcohol altogether or by making it more costly. Thus, the proposal of the SNP either restricts liberty more than what is necessary for its end (public order) or is, at least in part, intentionally paternalistic. Since the harms to others that arise from drinking can, it seems, be tackled by less intrusive measures and paternalistic reasons cannot, according to Mill, justify restricting someone's liberty, introducing a minimum price for alcohol would, for Mill, be an unjustified interference in people's freedom.

There is, however, one further twist in this tale. The Scottish government has repeatedly stressed that its minimum pricing policy is *not* a tax, presumably because that would be even less popular with voters. Had the policy been introduced as a tax, though, then Mill *might* have considered it justifiable. Shortly after arguing that the state ought not to increase the costs of certain activities *for the purpose of deterring competent adults from those activities*, Mill (1977) goes on to add

> it must be remembered that taxation for fiscal purposes is absolutely inevitable; that in most countries it is necessary that a considerable part of that taxation should be indirect; that the State, therefore, cannot help imposing penalties, which to some persons may be prohibitory, on the use of some articles of consumption. It is hence the duty of the State to consider, in the imposition of taxes, what commodities the consumers can best spare; and *a fortiori*, to select in preference those of which it deems the use, beyond a very moderate quantity, to be positively injurious. Taxation, therefore, of stimulants, up to the point which produces the largest amount of revenue (supposing that the State needs all revenue which it yields) is not only admissible, but to be approved of. (p. 298)

In other words, not all increases in costs are illegitimate: as with any other restriction, it all depends upon the justification. Mill (1977) allows that we may avoid those whose conduct we disapprove of and that this may amount to a penalty attached to their conduct, but this is legitimate because it is not purposely inflicted as punishment (p. 278). Simply attaching greater costs to some ways of life is not itself objectionable; we need to look at the reasons for doing this. The state cannot make alcohol more costly with the aim of discouraging people from drinking, but it can do so for the purpose of raising revenue.

I have argued that the harm principle rules out certain justifications for interfering in individual liberty. As noted above, however, this does not prohibit intervention that is *motivated* by paternalistic (or moralistic) reasons, provided that these measures can be given adequate justification that does not depend upon these excluded reasons. Mill suggests that raising necessary tax revenue is an appropriate justification for state action (presumably he sees this as necessary to preventing harms). Thus, a tax on alcohol can be justified as a means of raising income, and this is so even if the motivation of governors is to discourage drinking. In this case, the policy is justified as a means to raise revenue, while the effect of discouraging drinking is merely a side effect, albeit a welcome one.

4. Conclusion

I have considered a Millian response to the Scottish government's proposals for a minimum price on alcohol. While I have not, here, sought to defend Mill's conclusions, I believe it informative to consider what a leading figure in the liberal tradition would say about such proposals. My interpretive conclusion is that while Mill would allow the state to regulate the sale of alcohol in various ways, he would most likely regard a minimum price policy as illegitimate interference with the liberty of those who wish to drink. At the very least, he would entirely reject paternalistic reasons, which seem to play some role in the proposal of the SNP. While one might still seek to justify minimum pricing *solely* in terms of preventing harm to others, Mill would allow such a measure only if it was shown, first, that the social harm prevented was greater than the liberty lost *and*, second, that less costly alternatives were ineffective. The burden is on proponents of such restrictions to show that they are necessary and expedient. Justifying minimum pricing thus requires either meeting this burden or rejecting the Millian framework. Ironically, however, the same Millian reasoning suggests that the Scottish government might legitimately have been able to achieve its ends if it proposed a tax on alcohol, which could be justified as a means to raise revenue, without having to rely on paternalistic reasons.

Acknowledgements

I thank Andrea Baumeister and Danielle Wisbey for extensive discussions of this topic, Antony Duff for written comments on an earlier draft, and audiences in Glasgow (January 2012) and Stirling (February 2012) for helpful questions and feedback, particularly from Ben Colburn, Rowan Cruft, and Brian Ho.

Notes

1. This is, of course, a crucial concession. The proposal is not justified if not efficacious. Moreover, even if it would be efficacious, it would need to be shown that no less costly alternative would be (almost) as good.
2. This is true as an approximation. Since laws have to be framed in general terms, it may be that some harmless actions are prohibited by a law that aims to prevent harms. But this is a case where intervention is over-inclusive. This would not be legitimate if it were practical to prevent the harms without interfering in the harmless actions. I return to such issues below.
3. At least, not *logically* necessary. As an empiricist and a utilitarian, Mill's ultimate conclusions must rest on what proves efficacious. It might be shown that no other measures would in fact successfully prevent social harms that arise from drinking *and* that preventing these harms outweighs the loss of liberty that minimum pricing would entail. Then, and only then, would Mill be reconciled to such a proposal. Since questions of efficacy must be bracketed here, it is perhaps better to re-state my conclusion more moderately: for Mill, the presumption would be against minimum pricing, unless and until it was shown to (a) prevent more social harm than good and (b) be the least costly way of doing so. Any harm that drinkers do *to themselves*, however, would not be counted in these calculations.

4. We might deny this, for instance, pointing to the different expressive implications of increased price and a fine. But consumers do not always respond to these signals as the price- (or fine-) setters intend. If people regard a fine as a price, then they may be more likely to act in the undesirable way!

References

Arneson, R. (1980). Mill versus paternalism. *Ethics, 90,* 470–489.

Brink, D. (1992). Mill's deliberative utilitarianism. *Philosophy & Public Affairs, 21*, 67–103.

British Broadcasting Corporation. (2011). *SNP conference: Alcohol pricing bill back to Holyrood.* Retrieved February 29, 2012, from http://www.bbc.co.uk/news/uk-scotland-scotland-politics-15394208

British Broadcasting Corporation. (2012). *Minimum alcohol price planned for England and Wales.* Retrieved April 8, 2012, from http://www.bbc.co.uk/news/uk-17482035

Brown, A. (2008). The Racial and Religious Hatred Act 2006: A Millian response. *Critical Review of International Social and Political Philosophy, 11*, 1–24.

Burley, J. (2008). Mill, liberty, and (genetic) 'experiments in living'. In C.L. Ten (Ed.), *Mill's On Liberty: A critical guide* (pp. 185–208). Cambridge: Cambridge University Press.

Dyzenhaus, D. (1992). John Stuart Mill and the harm of pornography. *Ethics, 102*, 534–551.

Holtug, N. (2001). The harm principle and genetically modified food. *Journal of Agricultural and Environmental Ethics, 14*, 169–178.

Mill, J.S. (1977). On Liberty. In J.M. Robson (Ed.), *The collected works of John Stuart Mill, volume XVIII: Essays on politics and society, part 1* (213–310). Toronto: University of Toronto Press and London: Routledge and Kegan Paul.

Mill, J.S. (1985). Utilitarianism. In J.M. Robson (Ed.), *The collected works of John Stuart Mill, volume X: Essays on ethics, religion and society* (203–259). Toronto: University of Toronto Press and London: Routledge and Kegan Paul.

Moffat, R. (1998). Cloning freedom: Criminalization or empowerment in reproductive policy? *Valparaiso Law Review, 32*, 583–605.

Moffat, R. (2005). Not the law's business: The politics of tolerance and the enforcement of morality. *Florida Law Review, 57*, 1097–1133.

Mulgan, T. (2011). *Ethics for a broken world: Imagining philosophy after catastrophe.* Durham: Acumen.

Parmet, W. (2008). J.S. Mill and the American law of quarantine. *Public Health Ethics, 1*, 210–222.

Rawls, J. (2007). *Lectures on the history of political philosophy* (S. Freeman, Ed.). Cambridge, MA: Harvard University Press.

Rees, J. (1991). A re-reading of Mill On Liberty. In J. Gray & G.W. Smith (Eds.), *J.S. Mill On Liberty in focus* (pp. 169–189). London: Routledge.

Riley, J. (1991). One very simple principle. *Utilitas, 3*, 1–35.

Ripstein, A. (2006). Beyond the harm principle. *Philosophy and Public Affairs, 34*, 215–245.

Saunders, B. (2010). J.S. Mill's conception of utility. *Utilitas, 22*, 52–69.

Saunders, B. (2011). Reinterpreting the qualitative hedonism advanced by J.S. Mill. *Journal of Value Inquiry, 45*, 187–201.

Saunders, B. (n.d.). *Reformulating Mill's harm principle.* Unpublished manuscript.

Skorupski, J. (1989). *John Stuart Mill.* London and New York, NY: Routledge.

Steiner, H. (1994). *An essay on rights.* Oxford: Blackwell.

Sturgeon, N. (2010). Mill's hedonism. *Boston University Law Review, 90*, 1705–1729.

Tebbit, M. (2000). *Philosophy of law: An introduction.* London: Routledge.

Ten, C.L. (1980). *Mill On Liberty.* Oxford: Clarendon Press.

The Scottish Government. (n.d.). *Alcohol.* Retrieved February 28, 2012, from http://www.scotland.gov.uk/Topics/Health/health/Alcohol

Vernon, R. (1996). John Stuart Mill and pornography: Beyond the harm principle. *Ethics, 106*, 621–632.

Waldron, J. (1987). Mill and the value of moral distress. *Political Studies, 35*, 410–423.

Wollheim, R. (1973). John Stuart Mill and the limits of state action. *Social Research, 40*, 1–30.

Respectable drinkers, sensible drinking, serious leisure: single-malt whisky enthusiasts and the moral panic of irresponsible Others

Karl Spracklen

Carnegie Faculty, Leeds Metropolitan University, Cavendish Hall, Headingley Campus, Leeds, LS6 3QS, UK

In the public discourse of policy-makers and journalists, drinkers of (excessive) alcohol are portrayed either as irresponsible, immoral deviants or as gullible victims. In other words, the public discourse engenders a moral panic about alcohol-crazed individuals, who become what Cohen [1972. *Folk devil and moral panics*. London: Routledge] identifies as folk devils: the Other, abusing alcohol to create anti-social disorder. However, alcohol-drinking was, is and continues to be an everyday practice in the leisure lives of the majority of people in the UK. In this research article, I want to explore the serious leisure of whisky-tasting to provide a counter to the myth of the alcohol-drinker as folk devil, to try to construct a new public discourse of sensible drinking. I will draw on ethnographic work at whisky-tastings alongside interviews and analysis of on-line discourses. I show that participation in whisky-tasting events creates a safe space in which excessive amounts of alcohol are consumed, yet the norms of the particular habitus ensure that such drinking never leads to misbehaviour. In doing so, however, I will note that the respectability of whisky-drinking is associated with its masculine, white, privileged habitus – the folk devil becomes someone else, someone Other.

Introduction

If the British media and the discourse among the main political parties is any guide to the state of the Habermasian public sphere, there is a seemingly communicative consensus about the evils of alcohol-drinking. From tabloid to broadsheet to rolling news channels, state officials, health experts, academics (for example, see Room, 2004) and politicians condemn 'excessive' alcohol-drinking (Jayne, Valentine, & Holloway, 2008). But this consensus, while appearing as the result of a communicatively rational discussion, has all the makings of an instrumentalised moral panic designed to shift focus away from the machinations of global capitalism: the corporate interests in Government policy-making and the desire of the State to distract its citizens from the shifts in power upwards away from the democratic, communicative lifeworld.

In this article, I explore the serious leisure activity of single-malt whisky-tasting, whisky-collecting and whisky 'fandom' to provide a counter narrative to the myth of the alcohol-drinker as folk devil, to try to construct a new public discourse of sensible drinking. Single-malt whisky is whisky made in one distillery from malt, as opposed to other grains. For many years, single-malt whiskies were rarely sold and marketed by the whisky industry – instead, single-malt whiskies were predominantly mixed with grain whisky to make blends such as the

Famous Grouse or Bell's. These blends were a part of a modern, successful, globalising industry, and blends still account for the majority of volume sales across the world of whisky – but by the 1990s, whisky companies started to sell single-malt whiskies as a more 'authentic' brand, driven partly by enthusiasts expressing a preference for single malts and marketing teams eager to charge higher premiums for single-malt whisky (Spracklen, 2011). Whisky enthusiasts can collect rare single-malt whiskies, visit distilleries, compare the taste of different expressions from the same distillery, and attend regular festivals, commercial tastings and discuss their whisky knowledge on-line – single-malt whisky (and rare blends and single grains) has become part of the wider 'slow food' movement, with the tastings resembling those organised by the wine industry (Bertella, 2011).

The research in this article is partly reflective of my own ethnographic involvement in whisky-tastings over a period of two years, and my own position as a whisky enthusiast. The research draws on data gathered on-line and interviews with whisky-drinkers who attend tastings and those who just collect and/or enjoy drinking single-malt whisky. In the next section, I develop a theoretical framework about leisure that uses some Bourdieusian ideas (see Bourdieu, 1986) but is essentially aligned with Habermas. I then discuss the policy context and the literature on drinking-as-leisure, before briefly describing my methodological approach. Then I present three sections of analysis: one drawing on my ethnographic data, one using my interview data and one using data found on-line. I will show that participation in whisky-tasting events and whisky-drinking creates a safe space in which excessive amounts of alcohol are consumed, yet the norms of the particular *habitus* ensure that such drinking never leads to misbehaviour. In doing so, however, I will note that the respectability of whisky-drinking is associated with its masculine, white, privileged *habitus* – the folk devil becomes someone else, someone Other.

Theoretical framework

Stebbins (2009) has identified a kind of leisure activity he defines as 'serious leisure': an activity in which individuals become dedicated to the activity itself, or which becomes an unpaid career for the individuals. Stebbins is primarily thinking of the commitment people make to physical leisure activities such as climbing, which is rarely something done in a casual, *ad hoc* manner – or team sports such as rugby. But the concept of serious leisure can be removed from the psychology of leisure motivation and be applied in a looser sense to sociological analyses of leisure in its broadest sense. Individuals spend money and time on the leisure activities they enjoy because they identify a sense of self and a sense of community or belonging in that particular leisure activity. In our late modern society, serious leisure in this sociological sense can be used to resist the rationalisation of the workplace and the alienation associated with modernity: leisure lifestyles serve as a place of agency and self-realisation, whether individuals choose to be a fan of football or modern dance. Leisure is a place where individuals seek the liminal and the authentic, where they create liquid identities and intentionalities (Blackshaw, 2010; Rojek, 2010); or as Ken Roberts puts it, it is where people can be inconsequential (Roberts, 2011). In leisure, following Williams (1977), individuals adopt dominant and emerging cultural norms over taste, or choose to resist norms through the preservation of residual cultures. Following Bourdieu (1986), leisure is a key site in the formation of *habitus*, and a place where cultural capital can be accrued: a place where intersections of class, gender, nation and racialised identities converge. However, leisure theorists have also shown that the agency of choosing one form of leisure over another is never a free choice (Bramham, 2006): the decision to choose football instead of dance or whisky is, in modernity, the product of social structures, social inequalities and the dominance of global capitalism. So tourists who visit Scotland in search of authentic whisky distilleries have been tricked by a 'make-believe' Scottishness and a marketing sleight-of-hand into thinking they are making a discerning choice (Spracklen, 2011).

Leisure, then, is something of a paradox – on the one hand, it is by definition something to do with our free choices, away from the grind of the workplace, something that allows us to show off our individuality and the communities and cultures with which we identify ourselves. On the other hand, leisure has become part of the structures of modernity, one other place where we are given false choices or fooled into thinking we are free by the hegemonic powers that enslave us (Gramsci, 1971). The way to resolve this paradox is provided by the work of Habermas.

In *The structural transformation of the public sphere*, Habermas (1962) explores the historical origins of the Enlightenment and its role on the development of the public sphere. For Habermas, the public sphere is the part of society that emerges as a result of these greater liberties: people meet in coffee shops to discuss politics and philosophy; they read newspapers and political manifestoes and they identify themselves with the public, the people who have freedom and education to think for themselves and to demand more rights from the emerging nation-states they live in. In his later work, Habermas warns of the dangers of losing the public sphere and civil society and the threats posed to the public sphere by late modernity's twin evils: the bureaucratic nation-state and global capitalism. In *The philosophical discourse of modernity* (Habermas, 1985), he describes the different ways in which the idea of modernity becomes an all-encompassing shroud, befogging the reason of the public sphere. In *Time of transitions* (Habermas, 2001), he sees reason under attack from new forms of totalitarianism such as religious fundamentalism and nationalism. The weakening of this settlement and the growing globalisation of power is, for Habermas, a troubling symptom of the loss of the public sphere. When decisions on fiscal policies are made to serve the profit-making of off-shore banks and unaccountable trans-national corporations, something is clearly dysfunctional in the public sphere.

Communicative rationality for Habermas is emergent, contingent on actors and action, and dependent on consensus over the hermeneutics of language. Furthermore, communicative action takes place in what Habermas calls the lifeworld, which 'comprises a stock of shared assumptions and background knowledge, of shared reasons on the basis of which agents may reach consensus' (Finlayson, 2004, p. 52). Ideally, the lifeworld is constructed out of communicative rationality, which leads to principles of progress, fairness and ethics being part of that world. So Habermas (1983, 1991) argues in his analysis of discourse ethics and morality: the lifeworld is where reason and discourse shape laws about equality, for example, which can be seen in the way in which racial discrimination has been slowly challenged and criminalised in many liberal democracies. Against the lifeworld of communicative action and rationality, Habermas (1984, 1987) presents in *The theory of communicative action* what he calls the system: a symbolic construction that is created entirely from the workings of instrumentality on modernity. Instrumentality is purposive rationality and action, things done and ways of seeing the world imposed on us by the goal-seeking behaviour of actors and institutions that wish to limit our choice and our ability to get in the way of their goal-seeking.

Habermas' communicative rationality and instrumentality can be used to understand the meaning and purpose of leisure. The tension between communicative rationality and instrumentality is used by Morgan (2006) in his book *Why sports morally matter* to make a justification for the importance of sports participation. Morgan is concerned with the professionalisation of modern sport and the way in which modern sport has become driven by commerce. This is, he argues, a bad thing for the ethics of sport – but it is not the end of sport as an ethical sphere. Morgan argues that there is still the potential for sports participation to be something that instils social, moral and political values. This, he says, is due to the communicatively active nature of sports participation: people choose to take part in sports, choose to be communicative in their engagement in sport, and choose to adhere to internal rules about fair play. In *The meaning and purpose of leisure*, I attempt to challenge post-modern theories of leisure, and reconcile debates about agency and structure in leisure studies (Spracklen, 2009). Habermas is drawn upon to explain the so-called paradox of leisure – which it is clearly related to agency but also a product of instrumentality. I argue that leisure is something essentially communicative in nature, but that communicative nature has been undermined by the emergence of instrumental forms of leisure: leisure that is commercialised and commodified, which is provided by the State or by trans-national corporations to keep consumers docile (but content). Spracklen draws on examples from modern sport, pop music and the tourism industry to show that leisure activities at this moment in late modernity are sites for communicative resistance and instrumental colonisation: so, for example, 'extreme metal' music fans use their music scene to find communicative space to resist instrumentality, but they are also constrained by the hegemonic discourse of the music industry.

Public sphere – context and drinking-as-leisure

Robinson and Kenyon (2009) show that public moral outrage and hypocrisy over alcohol-drinking in this country is not a recent phenomenon: in the eighteenth and nineteenth centuries, politicians, journalists, academics and Christian moralisers campaigned strongly against the availability of cheap alcohol and its dangerous effect on the poor (who were caricatured as being unable to drink in a responsible manner). In the last 20 years, however, moral concerns about alcohol-drinking and the impact of such activity on individual and societal well-being have become the dominant way of thinking about alcohol (Room, 2004) – despite the pressure from the alcohol industry against regulation (Jayne et al., 2008; Robinson & Kenyon, 2009) and the hypocrisy of ex-members of infamous Oxford drinking clubs such as the Bullingdon telling others how much to drink. All political parties advocate tough action against those who drink excessively, and there is a political consensus that alcohol-drinking should be reduced and made 'disrespectable' in the same way cigarette smoking has been challenged (Jayne et al., 2008). Policy is driven by a combination of the health lobby and the morality of the *Daily Mail*. The public sphere is dominated by a narrative of 'failed' drinkers, rather like the 'failed' consumers of Bauman (2000) – people who do not have the power and knowledge to act 'sensibly' when consuming products and making lifestyle choices in the liquid modern. In the public discourse of policy-makers and journalists, drinkers of (excessive) alcohol are portrayed either as irresponsible, immoral deviants or as gullible victims (see, for example, UK Prime Minister David Cameron's recent moralising against the excessive drinking because of its supposed danger to the health of the nation and the economy, and the cost to the NHS: 'David Cameron vows to tackle binge drinking 'scandal'', on-line at http://www.bbc.co.uk/news/uk-politics-17036826, accessed 15 February 2012). In other words, the public discourse engenders a moral panic about alcohol-crazed individuals, who become – despite Critcher's (2011) argument that alcohol-drinkers are not a folk devil in the same league as terrorists or paedophiles – what Cohen (1972) identifies as folk devils: the Other, abusing alcohol to create anti-social disorder and long-term health problems.

However, alcohol-drinking was, is and continues to be an everyday practice in the leisure lives of the majority of people in the UK (Spracklen, 2011). Alcohol has always been a part of the everyday leisure lives of British people, and has dominated social and power relationships since the Middle Ages – but the advent of modernity saw the relationship change to a capitalist one. The development in the late-eighteenth century of industrial factories producing beer and gin led to a proliferation of drinking-houses in London. The factories could operate on a commercial scale because of the increasing application of technological advances in the production process, such as the use of steam-engines. Gin, in particular, proved cheap to make on an industrial scale once the technology of distillation allowed it – and, as a consequence, it became the subject of the first modern moral panic. Because of the cheap retail price and the high alcohol content, gin became associated with poor leisure choices: drunken idleness, cockfighting and bear-baiting, casual sex, gambling, fighting and petty crime (Critcher, 2011). Drinking, in London, had become a mass cultural pastime (Borsay, 2005; Greenaway, 2003) – and although the State tried to legislate against it, alcohol became a fixed part of the urban landscape, not just in London but in most other industrial cities in Europe.

The drinking of alcohol is a key leisure ritual, and in sport as in any other part of leisure where sociality is important, drinking and buying drinks is an accepted part of the subcultural practice. Alcohol's social function is evident in the cultural history of Europe and the UK: in the work of Mass Observation, for example, the pubs of 1930s and 1940s northern England provide spaces where men and women of similar classes are seen finding community and solidarity through rituals of buying rounds and indulging in light-hearted banter (Hubble, 2010). Drinking is part of the modern, Western quotidian – both a social lubricant and a matter of mundane habit (see the descriptions of the different drinking patterns in Newcastle in Hollands and Chatterton (2002)).

Methods

This research follows a discourse tracing approach (LeGreco & Tracy, 2009; Spracklen, 2011). Discourse tracing is a qualitative method of analysis through which it becomes possible to develop a 'thick' understanding of a given research focus. The researcher traces patterns across a range of qualitative data sources, developing in-depth knowledge of the object of the study, which in turn is used to make the multiple re-tracings of discourse, narrative, symbols, myths and attitudes. The focus of this research project is whisky-tasting events and whisky-drinking. Whisky-tasting events are where single-malt whisky enthusiasts are given a guided tasting of a number of whiskies. In previous research on whisky, I examined whisky tourism and the meaning of authenticity, using a range of ethnographic fieldwork and on-line ethnography (Spracklen, 2011). This earlier project also used discourse tracing but the nature of the discourses traced was different (as the data collection varied from the approach in this article). For the purposes of this research, I have reflected in an (auto)ethnographic manner on my own experiences of going to these whisky-tasting sessions, drawing on two years of attending 10 events. In addition, I have interviewed eight whisky-drinkers recruited through snowball sampling (whisky enthusiasts and those who have attended tastings), using a semi-structured interview technique and analysed the opinions of whisky enthusiasts published on a number of publicly available on-line blogs and forums, using both purposive searching and periodic lurking over four years.

Ethnographic reflections

> Springbank tasting, Feb 2012 – a large crowd of older, white men, leavened with a sprinkling of women (all here with male companions, husbands or partners?) and some younger, trendy types (glasses, humorous t-shirts).Our speaker is wearing a kilt, and describes one of the whiskies as tasting like Barr's American Cream Soda. In between drinks we get the story of Springbank – authentic history and mythology of timelessness (Springbank still uses malting shed to malt its own barleys, the family of the original founder still owns the distillery).

The whisky-tastings I have attended have all been organised by a wine and spirits shop in a northern town. It specialises in whisky and has run these tastings on a regular basis since 2004, beginning with two tastings each year and expanding to four each year, each with 80–90 paying guests. In the period of this research, I have been to eight tastings, missing two in the period of study: Bruichladdich (Scotland), Amrut (India), Bowmore (Scotland), Douglas Laing and Co (Independent Bottlers of Scottish Whisky), Glendronach and BenRiach (Scotland), Pernod Ricard (six Scottish whiskies from their portfolio of brands and distilleries); Springbank (Scotland) and Cooley (Ireland). In general, all these whisky-tasting sessions are polite. We drink lots (6–10 generous measures in the tastings and for most of the people there a pint or two beforehand to warm up) and we are eventually quite drunk, like our hosts. No one exhibits any anti-social behaviour, no one acts as if they are about to be sick (though of course people might get sick away from the venue). There is some rowdiness (cheers, jokes) but we internalise the good behaviour of the people around us. For example, at the Cooley tasting, the commercial director taking us through his portfolio of whiskies is keen to make jokes at the expense of Scottish whisky but his patter is constantly interrupted by good-natured banter and complicated questions from the crowd. All the time, despite the amount of alcohol consumed and the rising level of jocularity, most of the crowd are keen to take notes, compare the smell and taste of different samples, and listen politely or talk quietly. Whenever the talking gets too much, our hosts from the shop are quick to stand up and shout at people to quieten down – the manager even jokes that he has a list of people who are barred, but we all cheer at him before shutting up. For the Scottish distillers and companies there is an easy ride – they do not need to convince anyone in the room of their authenticity, fine taste and origins. Amrut and Cooley have to win over sceptics, those who are convinced the only proper whisky is Scottish whisky – they do this with some measure of success, but there are people at my table on both nights that are convinced neither India nor Ireland has anything that comes close to a renowned Scottish distillery such as Ardbeg or Macallan.

> Douglas Laing tasting, Nov 2010 – conspicuous consumption – the man next to me has bought hundreds of pounds of whisky. He is very nice and humble when we chat but he has just bought a bottle of everything. We learn to be snobs about single grains – they taste nice and they are expensive.

The whisky-tastings are of course a commercial enterprise. We pay a premium to attend the tastings, and the shop brings bottles of the whiskies that we taste to the venue, so we can buy as many as we like (at a reduced price). We have already proven our good taste by attending the event (we are reminded of this by all the speakers, who encourage us to explore the subtle differences between each whisky, and who constantly remind us that whisky is a spirit that takes time – three years at least – to mature). We can visibly demonstrate that with our choices of whisky at the sales table: buying the higher priced single malts or single grains rather than the blends, or justifying our purchases to each other over our post-tasting dinner. At each tasting I have attended, the people in the room are almost exclusively white, predominantly male and the majority look older than I am: the older white men seem to be divided equally between retirees and executive-looking types. Most of us feel able to spend money without worrying too much about the cost, but not all – there are a handful of retirees and others with more working-class accents who do only buy one bottle or none at all. As for the predominance of men at the tastings, that constructs a heteronormative value to the etiquette of tasting, which aligns with the norms of hegemonic masculinity: the majority of the men and about half of the women in the room drink all their whisky (the other women leave some whisky in the glasses at the end of the evening), even though whisky expert Jim Murray advises 'proper' tastings need to enforce the rule of spitting out the whisky to keep the taste sensors alert; and there is a marked reluctance to water down cask-strength measures (ABV 55–65%), even though doing so – to 'unlock' flavours masked by the high alcohol content – is recommended by every person invited to speak to us at the tastings. I count myself as someone who chooses to drink the cask-strength measures neat, even though I know it is not logical for me to do so – but then again, the cask-strength measures always come at the end of the evening, when my ability to act rationally is reduced by the drink and the 'clubbable' atmosphere.

> Cooley tasting, Apr 2012 – our speaker says Cooley has been bought out by Beam, an American corporation. He then says this means all Irish whisky is owned by a big multinational – Diageo owns Bushmills, and he says Pernod Ricard, the French, own Jameson's. He stresses the word French as if he is swearing, and the people in the room respond. Does anybody in the room like the French? he asks. I put my hand up but there is a round of booing.

My liberal inclination to like France comes from a love of French cinema, an interest in French philosophy and a slight envy of the status of culture and education in French society. This particular cultural capital sets me at odds with my fellow whisky enthusiasts. Their public display of displeasure at all things French may have been an over-reaction, and some of the jeers may have been due to peer pressure, but the simple fact is that it was perfectly normal for the crowd to express mild xenophobia against France and the French. The jeering at the Cooley tasting was not the first time this had happened – supposedly jocular jeering about France emerged when Pernod Ricard came to the whisky-tasting evenings. There is, then, a tension in this particular whisky-enthusiast circle. People are being expressively communicative in their desire to demonstrate Bourdieusian taste, through selecting whisky over vodka or gin, and choosing single malts over cheap blends. But the instrumental world of English middle culture emerges in instinctive reactions against France (along with Germany the country associated most with the foreign Europe 'beyond the channel' of the European Union) that bind the whisky enthusiasts to the political sphere of Middle England.

That said (or perhaps, because of that), there is among the crowd at these evenings a shared suspicion of trans-national corporations: Diageo, one of the world's biggest drinks companies, which owns the most Scottish distilleries, is regularly raised in conversations and questions to the speakers, and inevitably it is used as an example of overly aggressive takeovers, rationalisations and marketing strategies. While people drink whisky owned by trans-national corporations, including Diageo, they prefer to celebrate smaller whisky producers – independent bottlers are cheered as mavericks in an industry of global brands; and independent distillers such as Bruichladdich, Springbank and Glendronach/BenRiach seem to be able to do no wrong. These three, when they come to the whisky-tasting evening, make a big sales pitch to us that explicitly positions these companies against the faceless marketing executives or computer-operating process managers at Diageo: Bruichladdich is a working Victorian distillery saved by whisky buffs and Islay locals, and it employs dozens of local Islay people; Springbank remains unchanged since the nineteenth century, is situated in the deprived and unfashionable Campbelltown and is seemingly reluctant to sell its whisky and Glendronach/BenRiach is a company that now owns two distilleries discarded by the big companies. While the whisky enthusiasts at the tastings attempt to demonstrate they are able to express taste and preference objectively, regardless of the financial arrangements behind the distillery or the location, they inevitably favour whiskies with romantic stories of salvation, or those with 'genuine' traditions in romantic locations.

Whisky enthusiasts – interviews

Eight whisky enthusiasts were interviewed for this project: mostly middle/upper-middle class, all white, mostly male (one female respondent, one working-class respondent). Two of the eight (Respondent A and Respondent B) were a heterosexual couple in their late twenties/early thirties. The other six were older (Respondents C–H). The demographic profile of the respondents was designed specifically to map the demographic profile of those who attended the whisky-tastings. As respondent C identified about single-malt whisky:

> It definitely is more of a middle-class drink. That's down to price for one, for another that's about knowledge. Single malts haven't really been marketed to the mass market.
>
> Respondent F agreed:
>
> Some snobbishness about whisky – lots of money at the high end, pushing the prices up . . . lots of one-up-man's-ship about collecting. It's not just single malts, it's certain whiskies over others – being able to buy something at £120 rather than something at £35 from Tesco.

All the respondents collected whisky – mainly single malt but some single grains and luxury blends whisky and drank whisky on a regular basis: usually daily on an evening at home. The enthusiasts recognised that some whisky was for drinking on a daily basis, and some whisky in their collections, rarer bottles and those bottled at cask strength, were for special occasions: as Respondent B said, 'the Glenmorangie's for sipping, for guests, but the [distillery edition] Oban is my treat'. Drinking whisky, then, was something they did to relax, by themselves or in the company of close family and friends. Two of them did say they drank whisky at home on occasions to become drunk, but most of the respondents saw whisky-drinking as something pleasurable – the 'taste' of a good single malt – and relaxing – after a long day.

All the respondents viewed sampling and collecting single malts as an expression of their good taste – all argued strongly for their ability to differentiate good, 'proper' whiskies, especially single malts, from one another. And all claimed to be wise to the marketing of single malts and the 'dodgy' claims about authenticity made by some companies. As Respondent H explained:

> There's hype about some whiskies and some distilleries, you know really over-priced. You're paying for the packaging and it really surprises me that people fall for that, buying a whisky that's so mediocre they [the company] have to need to, y'know, all that like never judge a book by its cover, never buy a whisky cos it comes in a shiny box.
>
> Respondent D echoed the comments about marketing:
>
> Look at the advertising and the budgets the big boys have, Glenfiddich, Glenlivet, Diageo . . . they have to sell millions to balance the books, just like any brands these days. They have all these warehouses full of maturing stock and have to shift it somehow – fair play to them but I prefer to drink whiskies that speak for themselves.

There is a communicative rationality at work in the positioning of these whisky enthusiasts as serious, informed and sceptical consumers. They believe themselves to be knowledgeable about the whisky industry and the trends in whisky-collecting: they have accumulated the correct cultural capital to enable them to exist within the whisky field. They believe themselves to be aware of the tricks of the market and are cynical of multi-national corporations trying to sell them inauthentic whiskies. All eight have been to whisky distilleries in Scotland, and half of them have made two or more trips to Scotland specifically to visit distilleries. Six of the respondents have attended whisky-tastings or larger whisky festivals, and the other two are interested in going to one. All believed whisky-tastings and whisky-drinking more generally was 'respectable', something that was freely chosen and expressive of some communicative choice against the instrumental rationality of mass culture and global capitalism. In drinking whisky, they were positioning themselves against the excessive drinking, the commodified drinking, of anti-social Others:

> You learn from going to tastings that is okay to take your time, to enjoy the taste . . . (Respondent D)
>
> There's never any trouble at these [whisky] events.
> (Respondent H)

> You don't hear about whisky drinkers getting into fights in town. Drinking whisky is about enjoying the drink, understanding and respecting all of it.
> (Respondent F)

Finally, none of the respondents agreed with Jim Murray's assertion that individuals tasting more than one whisky in one session should spit out the whisky instead of swallowing it, but there was an even split on whether water should be added to whisky. For both of the younger couple and for two of the older respondents, watering down a cask-strength whisky to release more flavours seemed a sensible thing to do. But the other four respondents said they never watered down cask-strength whisky, preferring to drink it at its full-strength even though they acknowledge some of the flavour is lost. As Respondent E put it: 'I like the rawness of a cask-strength, it's whisky straight from the barrel, it's how it's meant to taste'.

Whisky enthusiasts – conversations on-line

On-line whisky discussion forums have been in part the subject of previous research (Spracklen, 2011). In this new research project, I explored a number of European whisky websites to investigate the dominant discourses around whisky-drinking/collecting and whisky-tasting: whiskywhiskywhisky.com, which includes a discussion forum; dramming.com, a self-styled independent blog; masterofmalt.com, a retailer that also hosts a blog; and caskstrength.net, a blog that is styled to appeal to youngish male urbanites. Unsurprisingly, given the nature of these websites, the discourses around whisky-drinking project a positivity and excitement about the whisky industry and the aesthetic pleasure of drinking a fine whisky (whether a deluxe blend, a single malt or a single grain). Caskstrength.net pushes a hip portrayal of sampling whiskies and cocktails and travelling the world, and the two bloggers who run the site are always fulsome in their tastings of rare whiskies. On whiskywhiskywhisky.com there is a competition between posters to demonstrate their superior knowledge and fine aesthetic judgement about different whiskies, with people using their avatars and signatures to publicly show their admiration for obscure or independent distilleries/expressions. Masterofmalt.com reviews whiskies that are usually available to buy from their shop, but they also comment on rare releases that will be out of the price range of most of their readers, or unavailable to the general public due to their rarity (most expensive whiskies never reach general sale as they are bought up by insiders and investors, who then re-sell on e-Bay with high mark ups – raising prices even higher – or who store their 'wealth' away like Dutch tulips). Dramming.com is unlike the other two blogs. Although the blogger who runs it likes his whisky, raves about the distilleries he admires and supports the whisky industry in general, he is also very critical of some of the practices in whisky: he is cynical of some of the marketing claims, suspicious of trends and hypes over rare whiskies and critical of whisky enthusiasts who buy into the myths of the industry.

On whisky-tasting, there are two general positions on the whisky forums and blogs – whisky-tasting is 'serious' but also whisky-tasting is 'fun'. Sometimes these characteristics go together but often there is a tension. The on-line debates construct and define taste and the norms and values of the serious whisky-drinker. For instance, on whiskywhiskywhisky.com, there were some interesting comments, the result of when someone posted as list of fifteen different whiskies that they were going to taste with a few friends (in the 'Whisky tasting with a few friends' discussion on whiskywhiskywhisky.com, on-line at http://www.whiskywhiskywhisky.com/forum/viewtopic.php?f=12&t=4758, first post 19 March 2011, 20.00, accessed 3 February 2012). One response (20 March 2011, 17.26, from someone identified as Malt-Teaser) was very clear about the danger of having too many whiskies to drink (all quotes *sic.*): 'I'd say this is too many to really enjoy or tastes them all in one tasting'. The implication was getting too drunk would spoil the enjoyment of the tasting. Another related pair of responses from the same person (20 March 2011, 18.14 and 19.03, from MacDeffe) argued otherwise:

> I would consider 15 a wee tasting . . . Remember, this is a tasting session, not a scientific analytic study. You want to sit around a group of friends and enjoy your self, have a good time and compare the drams. If you really want to go into depths of a dram I need to taste it many times over many days. I can often spend 1–2 hours on 1–2cl's. But hey, I drink like that when I am alone.

This led to a response from Olikli (20 March 2011, 19.13):

> When I 'taste' a whisky, I want to find out enough about it that I am able to publish a tasting note on my blog. What you describe I would prefer to call a casual 'dramming' session.

For MacDeffe and Olikli, the point of whisky-tasting in company was to be sociable, to get drunk, and to enjoy whisky and the good company. But they also recognised the importance (to them) of carefully analysing whiskies in a long 'scientific' session, which would help them with their own 'research'.

Discussion

The whisky industry – like the drinks industry – is a product of Western modernity. Whiskies became commodities at the end of the nineteenth century, produced in a rationalising network of modernised distilleries, warehouses, vatting plants, regional agents and sales offices. Through the last century and into this one, the whisky industry has ebbed and flowed with global fashions, with blended whisky becoming a standard spirit found everywhere alcohol is sold and consumed (Spracklen, 2011). Single-malt whisky is an expression of the Habermasian instrumentality of this industry. There is no pure whisky produced free from the balance-sheets of capitalism: every distillation is created with the demands of the market in mind, or rather, the expected demand (as whisky needs to mature for three years); every blend and single-cask whisky is sold to recoup profit and increase market share. The logic of instrumentality is evident in the recent history of Scottish distilleries. In the early 1980s, a number of distilleries were closed and demolished altogether – with no care for traditions and local economies – as multi-national corporations countered a surplus of whisky in the market. But when the markets changed the corporations changed. Single malts started to be sold directly to the market in significant numbers because corporations saw the success of some smaller distillers – United Distillers, the precursor of Diageo, branded six of its distilleries as 'Classic Malts' and invested resources marketing these distilleries as being representative of something authentic about Scottish single malt. Such marketing strategies continued into this century, with blends sold in emerging regions such as South America, India and China, and single malts sold at a premium to 'discerning' drinkers in established regions. In the last 10 years, new companies have entered the market, opening new distilleries or re-opening closed ones; and the corporations have responded with ever-more exclusive ranges of single malts.

Whisky enthusiasts are aware of this but still spend their money building up collections of their own – and they are still happy to buy single malts produced by corporations such as Diageo. In this respect, they buy into the instrumentality of their leisure activity, becoming Habermasian consumers of carefully monetised commodities. However, these enthusiasts do find some agency to use whisky-drinking and whisky-tasting as a communicative space. In the modern drinks industry, the hyper-commodification of global capitalism is evident in the packaging of lagers and flavoured cocktails aimed at young consumers – choosing to drink whisky, against the prevailing fashions and against the marketing campaigns for 'cooler' alcohol products, is a sign of communicative reason. Whisky enthusiasts are not drinking whisky to get drunk, they are drinking whisky because they like the taste and like to expand their knowledge of different whiskies. Engaging in discussions on-line and at tasting sessions about the relative merits of different whiskies is also evidence of a Habermasian public sphere, albeit a fragile one that is susceptible to colonisation from the industry.

In creating this public sphere where leisure is communicative, whisky enthusiasts are also constructing a particular Bourdieusian field, shaped by cultural capital about whisky and the white, middle-class *habitus* from which most whisky enthusiasts come. On on-line discourses and in informal conversations about whisky, status within the field is acquired by showing off one's rare and pure taste, one's distinction made free from the touch of marketing and hype. Enthusiasts who have never been able to afford to drink a wide range of rare single malts can always bluff, performing the role of the informed insider in some Goffmanesque play, but there is a danger in such pretence. Status within the field comes from actually having the rare bottles of Port Ellen in your collection, by being able to report that you have tasted them, or from visiting every distillery on Islay – but only those with economic capital can spend it. So the field and its associated *habitus* remain a site of elite privilege, associated with hegemonic notions of social identity, even if there is an associated communicative space.

This research does not present a generalised account of all single-malt whisky enthusiasts and all single-malt whisky-drinkers. The case study and the discourse-tracing approach only allow a sketch of some people's thoughts, conversations and actions when it comes to the buying and drinking of whisky. That said, the research presented in this article points towards a new approach to thinking about and the drinking of alcohol in modern society. Drinking alcohol is a part of many people's leisure lives. It is something people choose to do, something with which they fill their time and spend their money, something that allows them to meet friends or relax or feel a part of something bigger (Hollands & Chatterton, 2002; Robinson & Kenyon, 2009). Many of the whisky enthusiasts on this research situated their own drinking habits within the moralising discourse of public policy, legitimising their own alcohol consumption but being strongly critical of the teenage (pseudo) folk devils of the tabloid press (Cohen, 1972; Critcher, 2011). But the internal rules of whisky-tasting suggest that it is possible for modern humans to drink heavily but responsibly, getting drunk and getting merry but refraining from 'anti-social' actions. The policy debate will not change as a result of a handful of research articles questioning the norms of the limited moralities preached by Government and newspapers. But academics interested in alcohol-as-leisure need to move on from the stereotypes of abstinence propaganda – that alcohol-drinkers are incapable of control, that they are incapable of rational choice, that they are a danger to their own health.

Conclusions

We can see whisky-drinking and whisky-collecting/tasting is a leisure practice that challenges the moral discourse of alcohol-drinking in this country. It is a leisure practice that is communicative in nature – following Habermas, we can see that people construct their own rules, negotiate their involvement and attempt to keep a distance from the instrumentality of global capitalism. There is a confidence and assurance about their drinking and their collecting. However, the whisky-drinking *habitus* is one where access to cultural capital (*pace* Bourdieu) remains (almost) exclusive – whisky-collecting defines taste and belonging, but it also defines hegemonic whiteness, masculinity and socio-economic status.

References

Bauman, Z. (2000). *Liquid modernity*. Cambridge: Polity.
Bertella, G. (2011). Knowledge in food tourism: The case of Lofoten and Maremma Toscana. *Current Issues in Tourism*, *14*(4), 355–371.
Blackshaw, T. (2010). *Leisure*. London: Routledge.
Borsay, P. (2005). *A history of leisure*. Basingstoke: Palgrave.
Bourdieu, P. (1986). *Distinction*. London: Routledge.
Bramham, P. (2006). Hard and disappearing work: Making sense of the leisure project. *Leisure Studies*, *25*(4), 379–390.
Cohen, S. (1972). *Folk devil and moral panics*. London: Routledge.
Critcher, C. (2011). For a political economy of moral panics. *Crime, Media, Culture*, *7*(3), 259–275.
Finlayson, J. (2004). *Habermas*. Oxford: Oxford University Press.
Gramsci, A. (1971). *Selections from prison notebooks*. London: Lawrence and Wishart.
Greenaway, J. (2003). *Drink and British politics since 1830*. Basingstoke: Palgrave.
Habermas, J. (1962). *The structural transformation of the public sphere*. Cambridge: Polity.
Habermas, J. (1983). *Moral consciousness and communicative action*. Cambridge: Polity.
Habermas, J. (1984). *The theory of communicative action, volume one: Reason and the rationalization of society*. Cambridge: Polity.
Habermas, J. (1985). *The philosophical discourse of modernity*. Cambridge: Polity.
Habermas, J. (1987). *The theory of communicative action, volume two: The critique of functionalist reason*. Cambridge: Polity.
Habermas, J. (1991). *Justification and amplification*. Cambridge: Polity.
Habermas, J. (2001). *Time of transitions*. Cambridge: Polity.
Hollands, R., & Chatterton, P. (2002). Changing times for an industrial city. *CITY*, *6*, 291–315.
Hubble, N. (2010). *Mass Observation and everyday life: Culture, history, theory*. Basingstoke: Palgrave Macmillan.
Jayne, M., Valentine, G., & Holloway, S. (2008). Fluid boundaries - British binge drinking and European civility: Alcohol and the production and consumption of public space. *Space and Polity*, *12*(1), 81–100.
LeGreco, M., & Tracy, S. (2009). Discourse tracing as qualitative practice. *Qualitative Inquiry*, *15*(9), 1516–1543.
Morgan, W. (2006). *Why sports morally matter*. London: Routledge.
Roberts, K. (2011). Leisure: The importance of being inconsequential. *Leisure Studies*, *30*(1), 5–20.
Robinson, S., & Kenyon, A. (2009). *Ethics in the alcohol industry*. Basingstoke: Palgrave Macmillan.
Rojek, C. (2010). *The labour of leisure*. London: Sage.
Room, R. (2004). Disabling the public interest: Alcohol strategies and policies for England. *Addiction*, *99*(9), 1083–1089.
Spracklen, K. (2009). *The meaning and purpose of leisure*. Basingstoke: Palgrave Macmillan.
Spracklen, K. (2011). Dreaming of drams: Authenticity in Scottish whisky tourism as an expression of unresolved Habermasian rationalities. *Leisure Studies*, *30*(1), 99–116.
Stebbins, R. (2009). *Leisure and consumption*. Basingstoke: Palgrave Macmillan.
Williams, R. (1977). *Marxism in literature*. Oxford: Oxford University Press.

Storytelling: Walter Benjamin and recovery from alcoholism

Joel C. Beaupre

Department of Philosophy, Vanderbilt University, Nashville, USA

What follows is a critical review of alcoholism and recovery. The objective is to examine Benjamin's account of storytelling in light of the value of stories for recovering alcoholics. The research design is qualitative, and it is explained that, because storytelling requires experience of a vanishing sort, the design must be qualitative. The method is theoretical, drawing upon Benjamin's account of the societal changes that have brought about the disappearance of the storyteller such as the predominance of information. The main outcome is that the features of Benjamin's account of storytelling are evident in the body of experience that comprises recovery from alcoholism, but not in such a way that would suggest that his account of historical change is thereby null. In conclusion, the oases of storytelling in recovery provide evidence for the erosion of experience of the kind required to have stories.

If we conceive of the history of the social sciences as having branched between positivism and those rejecting positivism, then we can locate the figure of Walter Benjamin still only tangentially. The nature of the divide is of course as varied as those who offer reasons for it. It can, perhaps, most broadly be construed as a matter of the relevance of history to the practice of social science, but even to say 'the relevance' is to have already taken sides against those who would argue for no relevance at all. If we follow the 'historicist' branch of the divide (to borrow a term from its detractors), we eventually arrive at the critical theory to which Benjamin is associated, but even in this context Benjamin's notions regarding history appear wild.

For example, Benjamin (1968) claims that storytelling has been in a state of decline for a very long time, the first major symptom of which is the emergence of the novel (p. 87). 'Storytelling' here is not to be confused with the publishing industry and the 'short story', but rather is the manner in which experiences become counsel for others.[1] If storytelling is disappearing, then Benjamin's claims as to the unique features of storytelling should be increasingly difficult to verify. For where might one acquire a sample? As he tells us in Benjamin (1968), a critical vantage is predicated on the storyteller's disappearance: the 'dying out' of the narrative dimension of living speech is the condition for being able to see 'a new beauty in what is vanishing' (p. 87). Already in 1936, in his *Der Erzähler* (The Storyteller), Benjamin must reach back to the nineteenth century to find an exemplar in Leskov.

What makes Benjamin's account of storytelling worth considering by social scientists is that he appears to have understood something we might term the 'structural impossibility of experience' in its nascent forms. The kind of experience that is being lost (*Erfahrung*) is due to the rise of the isolated (hence exchangeable) individual (here one might go back to Luther), and the rise of information over the form of transmissibility peculiar to the story.

That Benjamin was able to discern the disappearance of experience is attributable, according to Adorno (1982), to his ability to actually have the so-called 'originary' experiences that had acquired mystical status among official philosophers (p. 229). Just as it took someone capable of experience to discern its disappearance, so too we might consider that it takes a storyteller to be able to understand storytelling.

This is not to suggest that Benjamin is a storyteller (he had aspirations as a literary critic and essayist), but rather to place a particular problem in view: If storytellers are disappearing, and if only storytellers can understand storytelling, then to understand storytelling is becoming an impossibility. Because narrative is disappearing in the realm of living speech, it is expected that there should be fewer and fewer storytellers around to tell us in what the art consists. Hence, whatever descriptions of storytelling are left are likely to be symptoms of storytelling's decline – when events, as Benjamin (1968) describes, arrive already 'shot through with explanation' (p. 89). Thus, it would be a great boon to find storytelling as part of living speech, for only then would it be possible to verify Benjamin's account of storytelling by experience.

To claim that narrative is disappearing in the realm of living speech is to claim that the conditions favourable to experience have changed. Storytelling requires a 'community of listeners' who are absorbed into the rhythm of (largely bygone) artisanship. The perpetually unfinished character and repetition of industrial labour made it impossible for people to have experiences, which depend upon being able to live through to the completion of something so that it can be seen in the round (p. 179). Benjamin states,

> In every case the storyteller is a man who has counsel for his readers. But if today 'having counsel' is beginning to have an old-fashioned ring, this is because the communicability of experience is decreasing. (p. 86)

If 'having counsel' was beginning to have an old-fashioned ring in Benjamin's 'today' of 1936, for us it is completely outdated. Anyone posing as 'having counsel' is likely to be a mere exponent of radically oversimplified pseudo-orientations to the world that are clung to out of egoweakness (Cf. Adorno, 1998, pp. 76, 111, 139).

Fortunately, storytelling survives (as the binding agent of a society no less), but where no one would willingly pay the price required to be able to retell the stories there. Storytelling persists today, but in the rooms of recovery from alcoholism.

Storytelling is the way a message of recovery from alcoholism is passed on to fellow sufferers: As its members say, recovery must be given away in order to keep it. But storytelling as a matter of recovery from alcoholism is not to be confused with storytelling that had been practiced as part of living speech. The time of storytelling is past: a time, says Benjamin (1968), when time did not matter (p. 93). Benjamin tells us that the perfection of a story is reached at a temporal limit beyond any single storyteller, the story having become a matter of tradition, which in turn depends upon the transmissibility of experience. In contrast, the premium placed upon the instantaneity of information need hardly be mentioned. Benjamin (1968) also observes that, unlike a story, information does not survive the moment when it was new, whereas a story does not expend itself (p. 90). Furthermore, counsel, unlike instruction, does not concern a relation of power (i.e. is not a command communicated between isolated individuals). In contrast, the social milieu of the story is a community with a gift for listening: in short, there is no such thing as an isolated experience.

The first element of Benjamin's account of storytelling that can be verified by the experience of the recovering alcoholic is of its relationship to dying. Benjamin (1968) recounts that people once predominantly died at home, and that the stuff of stories – one's life – first achieves a transmissible form as a result of dying (p. 94). The alcoholic in recovery not only has earned a seat by having escaped death, but also is advised at once to get a 'black suit' for the memorial services for those who will die. The real possibility of dying from alcoholism looms over each 'daily reprieve' from the illness. For the recovering alcoholic, the substance of one's life can be seen in the round as a result of having 'hit bottom'. The experience of utter defeat, so thoroughly alien to the defiant nature of the alcoholic, smashes the delusion of control over alcohol. The experience is, as with any experience proper, of a difference that is bodily undergone rather than chosen. In *Erfahrung*, the object breaks through subjective misrecognition and becomes cognizable in its difference. For the alcoholic, experience is the condition for a state of 'being teachable' without which no recovery is possible.

That the programme of Alcoholics Anonymous (AA) is a body of experience is particularly evident in the AA traditions, whose viable formulation evolved as the early society of AA met internal challenges that are particular to the socially misaligned character of the alcoholic. Not quite as evident, though essential, is the fact that it is only by experience that the steps acquire viable content. Even the most maligned tools of the programme, the slogans (e.g. 'one day at a time'), are merely placeholders for experiences without which no recovery is truly achieved. For the sake of the inexperienced alcoholic (who can only reasonably be expected to generate contrariness), they must be practiced 'on faith' until they acquire content particular to each recovering person. Only by acquiring content do they lose their hollow and false character; the slogans are redeemed as slogans only, insofar as they can be translated into experience.

Because storytelling is a thing of he past, we must understand storytelling in recovery differently, as a matter of survival from an illness whose causes must include the very social changes that Benjamin is concerned to track in the first case. The experience of the recovering alcoholic allows for an understanding of storytelling that the predominance of information otherwise banishes. For example, conditioned as we are to merely repeat the attitudes and opinions of contemporary individualism, the thought that 'experience is never isolated' should in fact sound strange. But to the recovering alcoholic, experience is passed down and enriched and then passed down again, and always a matter of collective experience. Benjamin (1968) observes that the lifetime back into which the storyteller reaches 'comprises not just his own experience but no little of the experience of others; what the storyteller knows from hearsay is added to his own' (p. 108). Recovery depends upon the ability of the recovering alcoholic, who habitually divides herself from help, to open up past the ideation that is but a symptom of the malady. This susceptibility to the counsel of others is first achieved through the astonishment that this ideation, believed by sufferers to distinguish them as individuals, is actually a shared trait.

Because the astonishment and thoughtfulness that accompanies listening is an experience, it becomes part of the life of the listener so that it can be retold. Benjamin (1968) states that...

> counsel is less an answer to a question than a proposal concerning the continuation of a story which is just unfolding. To seek this counsel one would first have to be able to tell the story. (Quite apart from the fact that a man is receptive to counsel only to the extent that he allows his situation to speak.) (p. 86)

For recovering alcoholics, the receptivity to counsel comes at a very high price. But one of the first gifts of this receptivity is a participation in stories that are unfolding in commonality with others. Stories instruct in ways that cannot be exhausted by assertions, nor translated without remainder into assertions. Benjamin (1968) states, 'Actually there is no story for which the question a to how it continued would not be legitimate' (p. 100).

For those who do not have a story of recovery, the danger of misconception is great, particularly in the way AA can appear to be bound by 'institutionalised' or inculcated beliefs. The typical suspicion is that AA claims in a disingenuous way not to be religious while clearly depending upon religious sentiments. That storytelling is the transmission of experience in a special sense creates difficulties for its study in ways not normally accounted for in typical research design.[2] A case in point is Rudy and Greil (1989), who argue that AA is a 'quasi-religion'. These researchers are bent on proper categorisation. They mean to capture what they describe as a tension in AA between the sacred and the secular. That is not to say that a description adequate to this tension is forthcoming. Their research begs the question as to the specific difference experienced by AA members between spiritual and religious. 'Quasi-' is really only a placeholder for the difference, which the researchers leave uncategorised.

As if spokespersons for the Enlightenment, their attribution of 'institutionalised awe' to AA members would reveal where superstition has yet to be bleached from the society by the light of reason. Having devolved to magic, religion today is universally suspect, not just inside the society of recovering alcoholics where, after all, one should expect illness (e.g. magical thinking).[3] If there can be such a thing as awe among such characteristically defiant and sceptical people, it occurs as gratitude for the discovery that there are others who suffer similarly and can offer real help. Real help comes in the form of challenge to the attempt to make religious belief substitute for practicing new behaviours. Only a programme of action, rather than belief, is effective: the 'disease' exists in the brain as a pleasure pathway that bypasses the higher cortex.[4] Consequently, one must 'act oneself into right thinking' rather than 'think oneself into right acting'.

Even as certain aspects of Benjamin's account of storytelling become visible as a matter of recovery from alcoholism, the stories that occur inside the rooms of recovery are not simple throwbacks. Instead, the damage to the communicability of experiences at large has resulted in alcoholism and other modes of escape. By coming to know something of the wounded oases of storytelling in AA, we encounter not just features of (otherwise bygone) storytelling described by Benjamin, but also the features of the age that creates the conditions for suffering. In connection to the damaged to experience of the wage-labourer, Benjamin (1968) discusses the gambler as the one who cannot have experiences (p. 179). Of course, the behaviours of 'getting and using' associated chemical addiction are just as perpetually incompletable. But that is not all. The worry that emerges from the work of Skinner (that we operate no differently than pigeons in reinforcement schedules) has been made the principle of industry. Today, we might think of addictive behaviour as having extended into all areas in which people are made to be susceptible to being drawn into modes of promised satisfaction in which real satisfaction is withheld. Where reality is bad, even the defiance that is usually a liability for the alcoholic is correct; only the self-defeating manner of defiance is to be changed. Real satisfaction would amount to a change in the conditions whereby one suffers. The erosion of experience is a form of suffering.

Notes

1. The industry surrounding the short story is a symptom of the change in time under discussion (p. 93).
2. Normal epistemological circumstances repress experience of the object for the sake of the research design. For the sake of ruling out experience as epistemologically bad subjectivity, the 'object' is sacrificed in advance to the framework built by the subjective intention. The operation of the research question that precisely controls what is to count as an answer is a residue of subjectivity. In contrast, objectivity in a precise sense would be an appearance that comes despite how subjectivity has equipped itself, as a moment of difference and a matter of undergoing.

3. Magical thinking is a component of the persistence of alcoholic behaviour, which is a form of dissociation from reality, a 'solution' to a current problem that presents itself to fantasy in absence of the ability to discern real and tangible options.
4. Consequently, learning and memory are impaired (cf. Adinof, 2004).

References

Adinof, B. (2004). Neurobiologic processes in drug reward and addiction. *Harvard Review of Psychiatry, 12*(6), 305–320.

Adorno, T. W. (1982). *Prisms* (Samuel and Shierry Weber, Trans., pp. 229–241). Cambridge, MA: MIT Press.

Adorno, T. W. (1998). *Critical models, interventions and catchwords* (H. W. Pickford, Trans.). New York: Columbia University Press.

Benjamin, W. (1968). The storyteller, reflections on the works of Nikolai Leskov. In (H. Zohn, Trans.), H. Arendt (Eds.), *Illuminations, essays and reflections* (pp. 83–108). New York: Schocken.

Rudy, D. R., & Greil, A. L. (1989). Is Alcoholics anonymous a religious organization? Meditations on marginality. *Sociology of Religion, 50*(1), 41–51.

Index

Note: Page numbers followed by 'n' refer to notes

For Product Safety Concerns and Information please contact our EU representative GPSR@taylorandfrancis.com Taylor & Francis Verlag GmbH, Kaufingerstraße 24, 80331 München, Germany